HUMAN BULLETS

A SOLDIER'S STORY OF PORT ARTHUR

BY

TADAYOSHI SAKURAI

LIEUTENANT I. J. A.

WITH AN INTRODUCTION BY COUNT OKUMA

TRANSLATED BY   EDITED BY

MASUJIRO HONDA   **ALICE MABEL BACON**

INTRODUCTION TO THE BISON BOOKS EDITION BY

ROGER SPILLER

UNIVERSITY OF NEBRASKA PRESS
LINCOLN AND LONDON

Introduction to the Bison Books Edition © 1999 by the
University of Nebraska Press
Manufactured in the United States of America

⊗

First Bison Books printing: 1999
Most recent printing indicated by the last digit below:
10   9   8   7   6   5   4   3   2   1

Library of Congress Cataloging-in-Publication Data
Sakurai, Tadayoshi, 1879–1965.
[Nikudan. English]
Human bullets: a soldier's story of Port Arthur / by Tadayoshi
Sakurai; with an introduction by Count Okuma; translated by
Masujiro Honda; edited by Alice Mabel Bacon; introduction to
the Bison books edition by Roger Spiller.
p.   cm.
ISBN 0-8032-9266-X (pbk.: alk. paper)
1. Port Arthur (China)—History—Siege, 1904–1905.
I. Okuma, Shigenobu, 1838–1922.   II. Honda, Masujiro.
III. Bacon, Alice Mabel, 1858–1918.   IV. Spiller, Roger J.
V. Title.
DS517.3.S24   1999
952.03′1—dc21
99-10482   CIP

Reprinted from the original 1907 edition by Houghton, Mifflin
and Co., Boston.

Introduction to the Bison Books Edition

Roger Spiller

The war that cost the author of this book his right arm began in the early hours of February 8, 1904. A Japanese fleet commanded by Admiral Heihachiro Togo launched a torpedo attack on the main body of the Russian Far East fleet, which was laying at anchor in the harbor at Port Arthur at the tip of Manchuria's Liaotung peninsula.

The Russians were surprised, certainly. In the days that followed, as news of the Russian declaration of war flashed to world capitals by wireless telegraphy. Official communiqués issuing from St. Petersburg sounded notes of genteel disappointment as if Japan had committed a breach of propriety. An Asiatic nation had presumed to challenge one of the world's Great Powers. But behind the professions of injury, one detects an overweening confidence: Japan may have stolen a march, but Imperial Russia would make short work of these curious upstarts. General Aleksei Kuropatkin, Czar Nicholas II's Minister of War since 1897, elected to take command of the army in the field himself. Kuropatkin sent a public word to those of his generals who were already in Manchuria, "Be patient, leave a little glory for the rest of us."

This much was true: Japan was an upstart in the society of nations. After several hundred years of determined isolation from the world beyond its shores, in the Meiji Restoration of 1868 Japan had inaugurated sweeping political and social reforms aimed at preparing itself for a new role in the international world. Outside, imperialism was running at high tide. Great Britain, France, Germany, Russia, even the Americans—upstarts themselves—increasingly saw the world as theirs to apportion between them, and all the Great Powers looked to Asia as the most promising of imperial frontiers. In a seemingly perpetual state of political disarray, China was especially attractive to Imperial Russia, whose Czarist government saw in the ports of China and Manchuria natural extensions of its Far East empire. Just as the century was about to turn, Japan's ambitions pointed toward the same regions.

Ten years before Togo's attack at Port Arthur, Imperial Japan had its first outing in a war against China to press a claim for hegemony over Korea and the Manchurian ports. Utterly incapable of resisting, China had capitulated promptly. But at Japan's moment of triumph, a coalition of Great Powers led by Russia intervened with diplomatic pressure and poorly disguised threats. Japan relinquished its newly won territory but not its memory. After a decade of nursing its resentments against Russia, Japan meant to renew its campaign for a colonial foothold on the Asian mainland.

By 1904, Port Arthur had become the most distant, and the most important outpost of Russia's imperial ambitions, a symbol of its power in the Far East. The harbor was Russia's only door to the warmer waters of the Pacific. Hundreds of miles to the north lay Vladivostok, Russia's other major port, but it was closed for much of the year by Admiral Winter. And while Vladivostok was barely accessible from either sea or land, Port Arthur was quickly developed as the terminus of Russia's grandest imperial project of all, the Trans-Siberian Railroad. As a mark of its importance, Port Arthur was defended not only by the fleet, but by thousands of garrison troops as well.

Port Arthur was as dreary, monotonous, and raw as the Siberian winds that swept over the barren hills of the peninsula. Since the Boxer Uprising of 1900, Russian troops had been patrolling the railway between Port Arthur and Mukdin against raids from bands of Chinese outlaws—"Huntuntzes," the Russians called them. For the troops, imperial policing was the order of the day, searching for enemies that mostly refused to be found. The thought that these troops and their commanders might one day meet an army much like themselves never troubled routine. No power worthy of the name could be seen on the horizon. And, after all, history sided with routine: no Asiatic power in memory recent or distant had dared to come out against a European army. Of course, the Russians knew Japan had been rebuilding its armed forces along Western lines for more than a generation, but any suggestion that the Japanese could fight modern armed forces on their own terms was regarded as laughable.

The transformation of the Japanese armed forces in the years after the Meiji Restoration is unique in the history of warfare—deliberate, disciplined, and true to its original conceptions. The long chivalric military traditions of Japan had turned on a feudal relationship between master and servitor, lord and samurai. Here as in feudal Europe, military power had devolved to a collection of clans, each dominating its own domain. Japan's new leaders understood that a new-model, national army—a critical building block in the construction of a modern nation—could not be founded on these ancient, particularistic ways. But neither was it possible, nor was it considered desirable, to wantonly discard centuries of martial tradition. Somehow, these ancient values must be translated into the service of a mass, national, Western-style army. Over the course of a dozen turbulent years, the power of provincial, clan lordship was redirected toward a new imperial system with a rejuvenated emperor as its embodiment. The elite values of the Code of Bushido by which the samurai lived were gradually infused into the new Imperial Japanese Army, so that the rawest country recruit might be made to feel a devotion to the Meiji Emperor as intense as a samurai of old felt toward his lord—a democratization of values on a grand, national scale. Aspirants to a professional soldier's life who under the old system would never have been permitted entrance, now filled new military schools to learn from foreign military instructors a modern, far more technical style of war than earlier generations had known. Improvements in training, organization and arms followed in due course. By the close of the century, the Imperial Japanese Army was hardly distinguishable from its Western counterparts, at least in appearance.

For the greater part of that century, armies everywhere puzzled over how to adapt to the tremendous violent power the Industrial Revolution had placed in their hands. New weapons fired more reliably and accurately, faster and at greater range than ever. The deadly zones of the modern battlefield grew apace, exposing soldiers to fire from ever greater distances. The dense formations of old, tight groupings of soldiers whose collective purpose was to throw their enemies into disorder by close range fire and physical shock were made to disperse, to open their formations. But the new, open formations posed new problems. How were these formations to be controlled so as to achieve their collective purpose? Still faced with the necessity to move quickly and effectively across the deadly zones, officers could not wholly surrender their control. How could officers aim their combat power toward the right place at the right time? Ivan Bloch, a Polish banker who in the 1890s produced an immense, analytical study of modern war, concluded that modern conditions made modern war impossible.

So a problem created by technology, other military writers concluded, was best solved by psychology. Armies could not shrink from one another even though the danger seemed greater than ever. The only answer seemed to be to press home one's attack against all odds. When neither side could hope for a material advantage, when all modern armies had attained technological and numerical parity, the human spirit was all that remained. The most distinguished Russian military writer of the day, General Mikhail Dragomirov, held that the soldier's spirit counted above all.

Dragomirov and other military writers before the Russo-Japanese War knew very well what their conclusions entailed: casualties on a scale unknown in war. The only way to mitigate high casualties was to press the attack with an irresistible speed and fury, an *offensiv a outrance* as the French would argue notoriously in the First World War, an attack to the bitter end. And, for such feats, a spirit superior to that of the enemy's, an *esprit de corps*, was an absolute necessity.

The martial traditions of Japan, grafted now upon its new-model army, seemed ready-made for this approach to modern war. All the work that had gone into the shaping of a national polity since the Meiji Restoration would come to fruition. Now, the people of Japan had been educated to believe they were members of a great, uni-racial family of which the Emperor himself was the embodiment. This bond between nation and Emperor created and sustained a collective national spirit—*Yamato-damashii*. Modern war might make its technical, physical demands upon those who fought, but when one was armed with *Yamato-damashii*, material considerations were of lesser consequence. The title Tadayoshi Sakurai chose for his memoir, *Nikudan*, or *Human Bullets*—a polite rendering of the word—eloquently expresses the role that Japanese soldiers saw themselves fulfilling. Like the samurai, they would banish from their minds all the normal human impulses in the extremities of danger posed by modern combat. They would fire themselves with abandon at their enemy.

Little of Tadayoshi Sakurai's life is known today, but he seems the perfect representative of this period in Japanese military history. He was born in the mountainous Ehime Prefecture of northwestern Japan in 1879. When the war began, Sakurai had already graduated from military school and embarked upon a career as a professional soldier in the infantry. By World War II, still well known for *Nikudan*, Sakurai was Major General in charge of the Imperial Japanese Army's department of propaganda, *shinbun han*.

Sakurai's army began mobilizing in early 1904, shortly after Admiral Togo had trapped the Russian fleet at Port Arthur. Once Togo won command of the Bay of Korea, Japanese transports landed troops at the Korean port of Chemulpo, better known to Western readers as Inchon, for an offensive across the Yalu River and into Manchuria. Toward the end of April, the Japanese had forced their way across the river against hasty and confused Russian defenses and moved against the city of Mukdin.

After the Russian fleet attempted several sorties against Admiral Togo's fleet, General Yasukata Oku's Second Army landed on the upper Liaotung peninsula with the aim of driving southward and taking Port Arthur itself. However, their advance was interrupted by a brief but very fierce battle for a series of hills called the Nan Shan heights that lay astride Oku's line of march. Here, both armies were to have a foretaste of the war to follow. A solitary Russian rifle regiment commanded by a talented officer of engineers, stood in the way. After repeated assaults against entrenched positions protected by quick-firing artillery, machine guns, searchlights, mines, ditches and wire, the Japanese finally took Nan Shan heights at a cost of four thousand five hundred casualties. The Japanese High Command, perhaps misled by memories of their easy campaign against Port Arthur ten years before, was dismayed by violence of the battle for Nan Shan. But the campaign for Port Arthur would continue, and the human cost for every inch of ground would increase.

Sakurai's infantry unit made its landing on the peninsula too late to participate in the assaults on Nan Shan heights. With the nervous enthusiasm common to all troops innocent of combat, Sakurai and his men hurried to join their comrades only to be disappointed. But on the heights after the battle, Sakurai saw for the first time the awful wreckage of men and equipment that were the hallmarks of modern combat. Perhaps here Sakurai also began to understand the true meaning of the phrase he and his comrades had been enjoined by their Emperor to remember: for a soldier of Imperial Japan, "duty is heavier than a mountain . . . death is lighter than a feather."

After Nan Shan more troops landed, and a new army was formed for the attack on Port Arthur. General Maresuke Nogi, recalled from retirement, arrived to assume command. During the war with China, Nogi's command had taken Port Arthur in one day with only sixteen casualties. Nogi was a romantic character, a modern soldier who possessed the *gravitas* of the samurai, and in this respect he was no poseur. His eldest son had already died at the battle for Nan Shan heights, and the war would take his only remaining son outside Port Arthur itself. When the Meiji Emperor finally died in 1912, Nogi would follow the old ways and commit ritual suicide. Although in 1904 he is a figure of some national prominence, there were those in his army who thought his technical military skills were unequal to the task. In modern war, they argued, spirituality is no substitute for professional competence.

The landward defenses of Port Arthur were formidable. The terrain seems made for defense. Barren hills, several hundred meters high, and deep ravines stood as barriers to the army's axis of advance. The Russians had emplaced three major defensive lines, and since the declaration of war they had collected more than five hundred artillery pieces, which had been fixed in heavily protected "bombproof" shelters. By July, when Sakurai and his comrades reached the outer defenses, there were eighty thousand of them, and they had nearly five hundred guns of their own. Forty thousand Russian troops, reinforced by sailors from the blockaded fleet, stood in defense.

But Nogi hardly seemed to know how to handle such an army, and over the next several months he ordered a succession of assaults against the Russian fortifications. During the fighting and siege that followed, Nogi's Third Army bled sixty thousand casualties. Demonstrating, if any demonstration were needed by now, the predominating power of the defense in modern war, Russian casualties would be half as many.

Sakurai became one of these casualty figures during the first general assault on Port Arthur, his right arm shattered by shell fire. True to predictions, Sakurai and his men were in danger from enemy fire at unheard-of ranges. Unable to stay alive as they approached enemy fortifications, they took cover behind the barest protection, sometimes only the corpses left from a previous attack. Soon enough, they began to dig their way forward, and the fight for each hillside position took on the character of a siege in miniature. Night offered the only protection, but even then soldiers inching their way forward were in danger of being caught in the searchlights the Russians had installed. Machine guns raked the wire perimeters that encircled most of the Russian positions. From August to December, the fighting continued until the most important of the Russian defenses at 203 Meter hill, fell after a day-long artillery bombardment and final assault. Port Arthur surrendered to General Nogi on January 2, 1905, but by then Sakurai had already made his payment for the victory.

Sakurai's service was over but the war continued elsewhere. In February 1905 one of the largest battles ever seen was fought to a stalemate at Mukdin. Each side then had over three hundred and ten thousand men arrayed in trench lines that stretched for more than forty miles. After nearly three weeks, the Russian army evacuated Mukdin and slowly marched northward toward Harbin. The Russians had lost one hundred thousand more casualties here. The Japanese lost eighty thousand of their own. Imperial Russia, seething with revolutionary discord, was in no mood to continue. The war ended at the negotiating table. The Treaty of Portsmouth left Japan in possession of Port Arthur and Manchuria.

As all modern wars have done, the Russo-Japanese War produced its share of memoirs, and in Japan, *Human Bullets* was something of a publishing phenomenon, selling forty thousand copies in its first year. Translated into English by Masajiro Sato and edited by Alice Mabel Bacon, a pioneer American educator in Japan, Sakurai's book was published by Houghton Mifflin in 1907 to favorable reviews in the United States and England. What no doubt made the book popular in Japan seemed to elude most Western reviewers. Sakurai's straightforward depiction of *Yamato-damashii* in action on the battlefields of Asia was treated as little more than a Japanese variant of national spirit. The war had been remarkable for the number of Western military observers and journalists it had attracted. Every one of these remarked upon the role played in the victory by the spirit of the Japanese troops, how psychology had triumphed over machine. Western observers, among them the British General Sir Ian Hamilton, saw in the Japanese a quality they feared was absent in their own armies and attributed its disappearance to modern industrial life. Few appreciated the deeply traditional roots of the *Yamato* spirit, and fewer still appreciated how this tradition had itself been so deliberately altered to assist in the building of modern Japan.

Sakurai enjoyed only a moment of literary fame. Despite the loss of his arm, he continued his career as a professional soldier, a career he shared with his writing. He produced several other works, including a commemorative book on General Nogi, but none captured the popular imagination as *Human Bullets* seems to have done. He died in 1965. Literary histories of modern Japan do not mention his name or his work. The few military historians who know of *Human Bullets* appreciate its unique view of the Japanese soldier at war in a time before his army became synonymous with the barbarities it committed in World War II. This new edition of *Human Bullets* renews Sakurai's contribution to an understanding of that army.

CONTENTS

EDITOR'S PREFACE

MUCH is being said just now about the Japanese as a war-loving nation, likely to become aggressors in the struggle for the control of the Pacific. This little book of Lieutenant Sakurai's will, perhaps, help to set us right in regard to the spirit in which the Japanese soldier fights. The story was told originally, not for a foreign audience, but to give to his own countrymen a true picture of the lives and deaths, the joys and sorrows, of the men who took Port Arthur. Its enthusiastic reception in Japan, where forty thousand copies were sold within the first year, is the justification of translator and editor in offering it to the American public.

The tale, so simply told, so vivid, so characteristically Japanese in spirit and in execution, is the work of a man of twenty-five who sees the world with all the glow and courage and enthusiasm of youth. Its honesty speaks in every line and word.

If, as seems now possible, the great new lesson set for the Twentieth Century is to be the meeting and mutual comprehension of Eastern and Western civilization and ideals, there can be no better text-book for us Americans than " Human Bullets," a revelation of the inmost feelings of a Japanese soldier of remarkable intelligence, spirituality, and power of expression. No better opportunity can be found for the study of Japanese psychology and for the gaining of a sympathetic insight into what the loyal sons of Japan love to call " Yamato-Damashii," the Spirit of Old Japan.

A. M. B.

INTRODUCTION

RECENTLY a retired officer of the Russian army and a correspondent of the "Russ" came to call upon me. When war broke out between Russia and Japan he was at Harbin; soon afterward he was summoned to Port Arthur and set out thither. But by that time communication had been cut off by our army, and in consequence he was obliged to return to Vladivostock. According to my visitor's story the railway trains from the Russian capital were loaded with decorations and prize money, and the officers and men traveling in the same trains were in the highest of spirits, as if they had been going through a triumphal arch after a victory accomplished. They seemed to believe that the civilized Russian army was to crush into pieces the half-civilized forces of Japan and that the glittering decorations and jingling gold were soon to be theirs. They did not entertain in the least the feeling with which a man enters a tiger's den or knocks at death's door. The Japanese fighters, on the contrary, marched bravely to the front, fully prepared to suffer agonies and sacrifice their lives for their sire and their country, with the determination of the true old warrior who went to war ready to die, and never expected to come back alive. The Russian army lacked harmony and coöperation between superiors and inferiors. Generals were haughty, and men weary; while officers were rich, soldiers were left hungry. Such relations are something like those between dogs and monkeys.[1] On the other hand, the Japanese army combined the strictest of discipline with the close friendship of comrades, as if they were all parents and sons, or brothers. Viewed from this standpoint, the success or failure of both armies might have been clearly foreseen even before the first battle. My Russian guest spoke thus, and his observations seem to the point.

The army of our country is strict in discipline and yet harmonious through its higher and lower ranks. The soldiers vie with each other in offering themselves on the altar of their country, the spirit of self-sacrifice prevails to a marked degree. This is the true characteristic of the race of Yamato. And in the siege of Port Arthur this sublime national spirit showed itself especially vigorous. Materially calculated, the loss and damage to our besieging army was enormous. If, however, the spiritual activity this great struggle entailed is

[1] Dogs and monkeys are proverbially unfriendly in Japan, as dogs and cats are with us.

taken into consideration, our gain was also immense, — it has added one great glory to the history of our race. Even the lowest of soldiers fought in battle-fields with unflinching courage, and faced death as if it were going home,[1] and yet the bravest were also the tenderest. Many a time they must have shed secret tears, overwhelmed with emotion, while standing in the rainfall of bullets. They respected and obeyed the dictates at once of honor and duty in all their service, and shouted Banzai to His Imperial Majesty at the moment of death. Their display of the true spirit of the Japanese Samurai is radically different from the behavior of men who appear on the fighting line with only the prospect of decorations and money before their eyes.

Lieutenant Sakurai is the younger brother of my friend Mr. Hikoichiro Sakurai. He had a personal share in the tragedy of Port Arthur and is a brave soldier with no little literary talent. I had read with interest the lieutenant's letters written while at the front, giving an inside view as well as an outside one of the war and describing the delicate workings of the human heart at such a time. Later I was very sorry to hear that he had been seriously wounded in the first general assault. He has written out the facts of the siege, with the left

[1] "Death is returning home." Quotation from the Chinese classics.

hand spared him by the enemy's shot. He tells us grand stories and sad stories, portrays the pathetic human nature in which fortitude and tears are woven together, and depicts to us the great living drama of Port Arthur, with his sympathetic pen. I must congratulate him on his success. To make clear the true cause of the unbroken series of successes vouchsafed to our Imperial Army, to make known to the public the loyalty and bravery of many a nameless hero, and thus to comfort the spirits of those countless patriots whose bones lie bleaching in the wilderness of Liaotung, is a kind of work for which we must largely depend upon such men as Lieutenant Sakurai, who have fought and who can write. He has blazed the way with marked success in this most interesting field of war literature.

SHIGENOBU OKUMA.

April, 1906.

AUTHOR'S PREFACE

THE Russo-Japanese War! This tremendous struggle is now happily at an end, and the hundreds of thousands of brave and loyal officers and men have come back from the fields with laurels on their heads, and welcomed by a grateful nation. What a triumphant air! How happy they look! But in their hearts is something behind the joy. At the back of their smiles lie hid the deep sorrow and the often forced-back tears for the multitudes of their comrades who, for the cause of their country and of His Majesty, have turned their bodies into the earth of lone Manchuria and cannot share in the delight of the triumphal return.

Toward the end of the Sinico-Japanese War, a certain detachment was ordered home, and before sailing paid a final visit to the graves of their dead comrades. One private stepped out of the ranks and stroked the tombstone of his special chum, saying with falling tears: —

"Dear Kato! I am going back to Japan. We have faced wind and rain together and fought in the hail-storm of bullets together, and you died instead of me, and I am going home in safety. I feel as if I were not doing right. I am very sad to leave you here alone — but be happy, dear Kato, Liaotung Peninsula is now ours! Your bones are buried in the Japanese soil. Be at ease. Understand, Kato? — I have to go."

He talked as if to a living friend. Every word was from the bottom of his heart, trying to comfort the departed spirit of his patriotic comrade. His loving bosom was full of a sense of the eternal separation of the living from the dead. He was silent and in tears for a while, then wiped his eyes and cheeks, offered water to the grave from his water bottle, and reluctantly resumed his place in the ranks.

That detachment who sailed home from Liaotung Peninsula a decade ago learned on their way that the peninsula was wrested from them. Poor Kato, who died with a smile for his country, did he die in vain? And was his heroism all for nothing? The rage and disappointment of his comforter may well be imagined, for after all loyal Kato's ashes were not buried in the Japanese soil.

For ten years we had been waiting and preparing for a chance of chastising the unjust. When the invincible Imperial Army first landed on that battle-ground of ten years before, how eagerly they must have been welcomed by the spirits of their dead friends who could not find a permanent rest buried in a place which was once theirs and then was not. When I landed on the peninsula and printed my footsteps on its earth, I cried out with a spontaneous joy: "This is also Japanese soil! Bought by the blood of our brave fellows at arms!"

I paid constant attention while at the front to find traces of those buried there during the previous war, but could not find even a rotten piece of wood marking such a spot. But I felt sure that their spirits were always with us and guiding us in the battles, stirring us up to do our very best for the country and for the sire.

"Beneath this your elder brothers' ashes are buried! Above here your comrades' spirits must be soaring, unable to find an eternal place of rest! Men die, but their souls do not perish. Your comrades in the world beyond are fighting with you in this great struggle!" were the words with which I used to stimulate men under my command.

Through the abundant grace of Heaven and the illustrious virtue of His Majesty, the Imperial forces defeated the great enemy both on land and sea. Our arms were crowned with an unparalleled success and our country with awe-inspiring dignity and world-wide glory. And the peninsula wrested from us is once more under our care, the neglected graves of those who perished in the unsuccessful struggle ten years ago are once more being properly attended to. The story of how over one million men left their homes and country, ready and willing to die for the great cause, and of how they passed eighteen months of hardship and privation among the mountains of Liaotung, on the plains of Manchuria, and on the waters of the Yellow Sea and the Sea of Japan, will forever be told to posterity in the history of our country.

The record of the great Russo-Japanese War will be written by the pens of able historians and writers. I simply as an insignificant fighter who took part in what may be called some of the hardest and ugliest battles in the annals of warfare and of strategy, of all times and of all nations, propose herein to describe with a hand not at all familiar with the holding of a pen, recollections of what I personally experienced and observed in the siege of Port Arthur, so that those who have not been in a similar position may picture to themselves the actual scene as best they can.

TADAYOSHI SAKURAI.

HUMAN BULLETS

Tadayoshi Sakurai
Lieutenant I. J. A.

MOBILIZATION

IN the second month of the thirty-seventh year of
Meiji,[1] the diplomatic relations between Japan
and Russia were severed, and the two nations began
hostilities. At the outset our navy dealt a stunning
blow to the Russian war vessels at Chemulpo and
off Port Arthur. His August Majesty issued a proclamation of war. Mobilization orders were issued
to different divisions of the army. At this moment
we, the soldiers of Japan, all felt our bones crackle
and our blood boil up, ready to give vent to a long-
stored energy. Mobilization! How sweetly the word
gladdened our hearts, how impatiently we waited to
be ordered to the front! What division was mobilized
to-day? What one will have its turn to-morrow?
How long shall we have to wait? May the order
come at once! May we find ourselves in the field
without delay! Not that we wished to distinguish ourselves and win honors in the early battles,
but that we hated the idea of arriving at the scene
after other divisions had borne all the burden of the

---

[1] *Meiji* (Enlightenment). The era beginning with the reign of
the present emperor.

肉弾 first struggle. But what could we do without Imperial orders? We were soldiers always ready to "jump into water and fire at the Great Sire's word of command."[1] We had to wait for the word "Advance!" How eagerly we watched for that single word, for that order of mobilization, as drought-suffering farmers watch for a rain-cloud in the sky! We offered "mobilization prayers" as they offer "rain prayers." Wherever we went, whomsoever we met, we talked of nothing but mobilization. At last about the middle of April, the month of cherry-blossoms,[2] emblematic of the spirit of Japan's warriors, our division received this longed-for order. Ordered to the front! Our garrison was granted the golden opportunity of untrammeled activity. I was at that time the standard-bearer of the regiment. I said to our commander on hearing this glad news: "Hearty congratulations, Colonel; we have just received the order."

Upon which Colonel Aoki smiled a smile indescribably happy as if he welcomed the order and exclaimed, "It has come at last!"

That was the happiest day we had ever experienced, and I could not help going around, half in frenzy, to the officers of all the companies to carry the news to them. A mysterious kind of spiritual

[1] Quoted from a war-song.

[2] The cherry-blossom is the flower of the warrior, because of its beauty, its short life, and its glorious death.

4

electricity seemed to permeate the whole garrison,
composed of the flower of the "Land of the Gods."
Every one, both officers and privates, seemed ready
to fight the whole of Russia single-handed. Our
souls were already on the great stage of Liaotung,
while our bodies still remained in our own country.

The men of the first and second Reserve were
none the less anxious and quick to gather round their
standard. Some of them were so poor that their
wives and children seemed likely to starve without
them, others came from the sick beds of old, dying
parents;— all must have had cares and anxieties to
detain them. But now the emergency had arisen,
and the time had come for them to " offer themselves courageously for the State." [1] What a privilege, they all thought, for a man to be permitted to
give his life for the nation's cause! When we saw
them swarm together day after day, our hearts
bounded with redoubled joy and strength.

Here is a sad story of this time. Nakamura, a
private of the first Reserve, had an invalid wife and
a baby of three. They were extremely poor, and
the family would starve without the husband. Of
course, however, the family trouble had no place
in their minds before a national crisis. On the eve

[1] Quoted from the Imperial Rescript on Education. This may
be called the Japanese Gospel on Education, and is read with all
possible tokens of reverence in all Japanese schools on all ceremonial occasions. For full text, see Appendix A.

of her husband's departure, the poor emaciated woman gathered all her scanty strength, went to the town near by and bought two *go*[1] of rice and one *sen*[2] worth of fuel. This handful of grain and bundle of firewood, are they really as insignificant as they seem to be? Nay, the two *go* of rice and the *sen* worth of wood were for the loving wife's farewell banquet[3] in honor of her husband's great opportunity. And yet at the time of separation, the wife was sick and the child starving, and the husband going to give his life to his country! In the morning, before daybreak, Nakamura bade good-by to wife and baby, and without a farewell from his neighbors hastened bravely to his post. Such was only one out of hundreds of thousands of similar heartrending instances. The kind and sympathetic people left at home at once began to relieve these unfortunate families, so that the men at the front could devote their whole attention and energy to their duties as soldiers.

When the men of the first and second Reserve arrived in their garrison, some of them were rejected on account of insufficient health or physique. How sad and crestfallen they looked when thus rejected! "Please, can't you take me in some way?

---

[1] *Go*, a measure of capacity equal to a little more than a gill.

[2] *Sen*, equal to half a cent.

[3] Rice is a banquet to people so poor that they live ordinarily on millet.

They gave me such a great send-off when I left the village, they *banzaied* [1] me over and over again when my train started. I came here determined not to go home again. How can I stand the disgrace of going back to my neighbors as a useless failure? Do please take me with you," they would entreat. The officers in charge had great difficulty in soothing and comforting these "failures" and persuading them to go home.

"Good luck to you! Your family will be well taken care of. All right, eh?"

"All right, all right! I will bring you a dozen or two of the Russkies' heads when I come back!"

"My dear Saku, don't die of an illness; if you die, die on the battle-field. Don't worry about your brother!"

"I am ready not to tread on the soil of Japan again with this pair of legs. [2] Be happy with me, when you hear that I died in battle."

"Thank you all for seeing me off so kindly. I will return your kindness by distinguishing myself in the field."

Words like these sounded at the doorways of the barracks everywhere. The men anxious to serve; the nation to help their families; was this not the secret of our splendid victory?

---

[1] "Banzai!" "Hurrah!" (Literally, "Ten thousand years!")
[2] This refers, not as it may seem, to the thought of coming back disabled, but to the idea of returning without the body after death.

第一

肉
彈　　We were busy night and day until the mobilizing was completed. Some were assigned to field regiments, others were put on the waiting-list, and soon we were ready to start at a moment's notice.

Those who were left at home to fill up vacancies later on were sorely disappointed, and entreated their officers to allow them to join the fighting regiments at once. Their comrades had to comfort and encourage, cheer and praise these disappointed men, explaining to them that the war with Russia was not likely to come to an end in six months or even in a year; that their turn was sure to come before long; that it was not at all a disgrace to be on the waiting-list, on the contrary that they were to have the honor of dealing the finishing stroke to the enemy.

After our regiment was ready to start, one sad affair took place. Togo Miyatake was one of those who were lodged in a Buddhist temple called Kwan-nonji to wait for a later summons. He was in good health and excellent spirits. When leaving home he had promised his parents, brothers, and friends that he would be among the first to help win battles. Now, instead of dying in the field, he had to wait, doing nothing. He did not know when he would be sent. This was too great a humiliation for him to bear. He thought it better to kill himself, so that his spirit, freed from the shackles of the body, might be at the front to work with his living comrades.

8

Left in such a situation as he was, poor Togo's narrow but strong sense of patriotism made him resolve on suicide as the most honorable way of escape. Late one night when his friends were fast asleep he scribbled a line of farewell to this effect:

"I am more sorry than I can possibly bear not to be at the front with the others. No one would take me in spite of my entreaties. I will prove my loyalty with death."

Thus prepared, he drew a dagger from a white-wood sheath[1] and cut across the abdomen, whispering Banzai to the Emperor in a shower of tears. This took place on the 12th of May in a lonely corner of an old tottering temple, when the sound of rain dripping from the eaves made the sad scene still sadder. But good Heaven seemed to take compassion on such a faithful soldier. His friends awoke and came to the rescue. He was sent to a hospital. His wound healed in due time, he was discharged, and later he was allowed to go to the front. Cold reason may call this man a fool, or a fanatic, but his heart was pure and true. This incident testifies to the childlike simplicity of devotion that prevailed throughout the whole army.

Russia prided herself on her vast territory and immense soldiery, but her people did not believe in the Czar's virtue. They were oppressed and

[1] The sheath and hilt of whitewood indicates the ceremonial dagger used in committing hara-kiri.

trampled upon by his ministers and officials. They were therefore not at all anxious to support the government in this war. Cossacks had to drive the unwilling men to Manchuria at the point of the bayonet. Yes, Russian fighters were brave and strong, but lacking in morale, the first requisite of a successful war. We, on the contrary, had an invincible spirit called *Yamato-damashii*,[1] disciplined under the strict rules of military training.

All the manifold details of business connected with mobilization were prosecuted with mechanical exactness and promptitude, as had been previously planned out. Everything was now ready and we were all eagerly waiting for the day of departure.

What an exciting happy time we had, while thus waiting and watching! We stroked our arms, itching for action, sharpened our swords, pictured to ourselves what we would do on the actual battle-field. Many a soldier must have flourished his glittering sword, as I did, and smiled significantly in the midnight moonlight of the quiet garrison ground.

When all necessary preparations were finished, our colonel put us through an armed inspection. The large drill-ground from one end to the other

---

[1] *Yamato-damashii*, the spirit of Yamato, an expression that contains in itself the idea of all that is heroic in Japanese history and character. Yamato was the province first conquered by Jimmu Tenno, and where he established his empire. The name is still used for that province, and poetically, to mean all Japan.

was filled with thousands of men and officers, each provided with his outfit, — arms, food, clothing and so on. Soon they were to brave, shoulder to shoulder, flying shot and thundering noise, pestilential rain and poisonous fog, eating together and sleeping together as comrades and brothers in danger and privation.

To the stirring sound of trumpets, our famous regimental flag was brought to the centre and an imposing ceremony of welcome to the flag was conducted by Colonel Aoki. The lives of the brave three thousand gathered round him were all in his hands. He has since told me that he was overwhelmed with a sense of great responsibility and with a feeling of proud exhilaration when he saw on that occasion how eager and ready they all were. At the conclusion of this ceremony our commander gave us a speech of instruction, in such thrilling words as made us bite our lips and tremble with emotion.

At the conclusion of such an armed inspection a few days later, Brigadier-General Yamanaka, then in command of our brigade, gave us a written piece of advice, in which the following words were contained:—

"The flag of your regiment has already won a glorious name in the Japan-China War. Its fame is impressed upon the minds of all. You have the responsibility of keeping this honor unsullied. You

11

are in duty bound to add to its splendor. And whether you will do so or not, solely depends upon your determination. Remember, that if you once bring a spot of disgrace upon the flag an opportunity of washing it away will not easily come. Do not destroy by a single failure the honor which your flag has retained since its first battle. I deem it my highest glory to share in ups and downs, to live and die with you officers and men beneath this historic flag.

"We are the main support[1] of His Majesty, guardians of the safety of our country. The only way we can fulfill our grave responsibility is always to remember the five items of his August Rescript;[2] to do our duty with sincere devotion; and to put into practice the sworn resolutions of our hearts. Our Emperor has now given us another instruction, saying,[3] 'We rely upon your loyalty and bravery in achieving this end (victory) and keeping unsullied the glory of our Empire.' How shall we respond to these gracious words of His Majesty? I with you shall put forth every energy to bring

[1] *Koto*, the Japanese word used here, means, literally, "arms and legs."

[2] Quoted from the Imperial Rescript to the Army and Navy upon which the moral education of the military and naval men of Japan is founded. For the full text, and the five articles, see Appendix B.

[3] Quoted from the Imperial Declaration of War against Russia. For full text see Appendix C.

this great struggle to a speedy and successful termination, so that we may make good the nation's
trust in us, and relieve His Gracious Heart of
anxiety. If we can thus secure for our country a
permanent peace, our humble efforts will be amply
rewarded."

Our already grave position was made tenfold
graver by this implicit trust put on us by His
Majesty and the nation. How did we bear this
tremendous weight of duty and responsibility?

OUR DEPARTURE

ABOUT a month after the mobilization was ordered, another happy day came to us; the 21st of May, a day we shall never forget to the end of our lives.

While we had been waiting for this day, we had heard news of repeated victories of our forces in and around Chiu-lien-cheng.

We were frantically joyous over the news, but at the same time could not help feeling a foolish anxiety. "If they were making such steady progress out there, might not the war be at an end by the time we were starting for the front? A certain division was to go in a few days. When should we have our turn? While we were kept idle, other divisions might monopolize all the victories there could be. No room would be left for us unless we hurried up!" So, therefore, when we received the welcome order, there was none who was not quite ready to start at once.

On that long-looked-for day, we were ordered to assemble on the parade ground at six o'clock in the morning.

14

Our joy was boundless, the time had come at last for the greatest action of our lives. "The brave man is not without tears, but those tears are not shed in the moment of separation," so the expression goes. Of course, we were as ready and willing to welcome the worst as the best, but because of this very resolve and expectation we could not help thinking of eternal separation, — parent from child, man from wife, and brother from sister. "Tears even in the eyes of an *oni*." [1] How could we be without unseen tears, though valiantly forced back under a cheerful smile!

On the night previous to departure, I took out my old friends' photographs to look at, made tidy the drawers of my desk, and so arranged everything that my affairs would be quite clear to my surviving friends. And then I went to sleep my last sleep on the mats peacefully and contentedly.

At three o'clock in the morning, the cannon roared three times from the tower of the castle. I jumped out of bed, cleansed my person with pure water, donned the best of my uniforms, bowed to the east where the great Sire resides, solemnly read his Proclamation of War, and told His Majesty that his humble subject was just starting to the front. When I offered my last prayers—the last, I then believed they were — before the family shrine of my ancestors, I felt a thrill going all through me, as if they

[1] *Oni*, a goblin or devil.

were giving me a solemn injunction, saying, "Thou art not thy own. For His Majesty's sake, thou shalt go to save the nation from calamity, ready to bear even the crushing of thy bones, and the tearing of thy flesh. Disgrace not thy ancestors by an act of cowardice." My family and relatives gathered around me to give me a farewell cup of *saké*, and to congratulate me on my joyous start.

"Don't worry at all about your home affairs — put into practice all your long-cherished good resolutions. For your death your father is quite ready. Add a flower of honor to our family name by distinguished service to the country." This from my father.

"Please, sir, don't be anxious about me. This is the greatest opportunity a soldier can possibly have. Only, do take good care of your delicate self." This from myself.

Such an exchange of sentiments between father and son must have taken place almost simultaneously in a great many families.

When the time had come for me to start, I took up and put on the sword that had been placed in the family shrine, drank the farewell cup of water [1]

[1] The farewell cup of water (*mizu-sakazuki*, "water-wine-cup"), to which reference is made frequently in Lieutenant Sakurai's story, is a religious ceremony, probably of Shinto origin, of the nature of a sacrament. At the moment of death, the nearest relative present administers water to the dying person, an act of purification for the next life. Hence, on the departure of

my dear mother had filled, and left my home with
light heart and light feet, expecting to cross its
threshold no more.

One officer was just going to the front in high
spirits when, on the night previous to his departure,
his beloved wife died, leaving a little baby behind.
He had, however, no time to see her laid in her last
place of rest. Bravely, though with tears hardly
suppressed, he started early in the morning. Private
sorrow must give way before national calamity,
but human nature remains the same forever. This
unfortunate officer's sad dreams in camp must
have frequently wandered around the pole[1] marking her burial-place, and about the pillow of the
baby crying after its mother.

any member of the family on an errand to which he has vowed
his life, the farewell cup that is given him is not the *saké*, typi-
fying joy and good-fellowship, but water, the symbol of purification. In one of the Japanese classical dramas, *Taikoki*, the
scenes of which are laid in the time of Hideyoshi, the Taiko
(1582–98 A. D.), a young man is about to depart on a forlorn
hope, with the certainty of ending his life in battle. He is be-
trothed, and before he leaves his home the wedding is cele-
brated; but the marriage cup which bride and bridegroom share
is filled with water instead of *saké*, as a sign that the union is
not for this life but for the next. The bridegroom leaves immediately after the ceremony and dies fighting; the young wife at once
commits suicide and rejoins him in the new life to which they
pledged themselves in the " death-cup" of their wedding-day.

[1] The mark over a grave, for a year after burial, is a wooden
post, cut square, and bearing the name, and the posthumous
Buddhistic name, of the deceased. At the end of the year, a
stone is substituted for the post.

肉
弾

At 6 A. M. our regiment was drawn up in array, the regimental flag was welcomed to the solemn and majestic tune of "Ashibiki," and we all looked expectantly toward our colonel, who was to guide us through "savage sands and barbarian winds." [1] The brave soldiers felt themselves to be the hands and feet of the commander. We had all said good-by to parents and homes: henceforward, our commander was to be our father, the boundless plain of Manchuria our home. Words utterly fail to describe that sense of mutual dependence which we felt at this moment toward each other, the one to command and the other to obey.

The colonel gazed down the ranks from one end to the other and read aloud his last instructions before leaving the home-land. Then at his initiative we *banzaied* His Majesty the Highest Commander three times over at the tops of our voices.

"Ah! a group of strong warriors has arisen! they rival each other in achievements of arms at the word of our great Sire. Where they go, the heavens will open and the earth crumble!" [2]

"First battalion, forward march!"

This was the first word of command Colonel Aoki gave his subordinates at their departure to the front. His voice confirmed our resolution to go forward,

---

[1] A classical Chinese expression meaning war.
[2] Quoted from a war-song.

and brave, at his order, the strongest parapet or 第二
the fiercest fire of the enemy.

Our long-drawn, serpent-like regiment, sent off
with the hearty and sincere Banzai of the people,
began to move on step by step. The noise of our
marching feet becoming fainter and fainter in the
distance, the sound of our rifles and swords softly
rubbing against our clothes, how gallant and stirring these must have sounded to the enthusiastic
ears of the nation! The trumpet that resounded
from near and far was our "good-by" to our dear
countrymen. Old and young, waving the national
flag and shouting Banzai in thunder-like chorus,
made us the more determined to deserve their
gratitude. Whenever in the field we made a furious
assault, we felt as if this chorus of Banzai were surging from behind to stimulate and encourage us.
Our own war-cry may well be said to have been an
echo of this national enthusiasm. In the morning
on the battle-field amid ear-rending cannon roar,
in the chilly evening of a field encampment, this
cry of Banzai from the heart of the whole nation
was always present with us.

My humble self was honored with the important
duty of bearing the regimental standard. The low
bows and enthusiastic cheers at the sight of the
flag, from crowds of people standing by the road-
sides, stirred my spirits more and more, and also
made me fear lest I might fail in my duty. Dur-

19

肉
彈

ing our march, Mr. Kojima, who had instructed me for five years in the high school, noticed me, came forward two or three steps, from among the watching crowd, with overwhelming joy in his face, and whispered in my ear: "Strive hard, Sakurai."

This brief but forcible exhortation from my kind teacher rang in my ears throughout the campaign and urged me to be worthy of his teaching.

War-songs sung by groups of innocent kindergarten-children — how they shook our hearts from the foundation! Old women bowed with age would rub rosaries between their palms, muttering prayers, and saying: "Our great Buddha will take care of you! Do your best for us, Mr. Soldiers." How pathetically their zeal impressed us!

Our transports, the Kagoshima Maru, the Yawata Maru, etc., were seen at anchor in the offing. The men began to go on board. Sampans, going and coming, covered the sea. Along the shore, the hills were black with men, women, and children from village and town, waving the national flag and crying Banzai at the tops of their voices. The farewell hand-shake of our colonel and the Governor of Ehime-Ken added to the impressive scene.

When all were on board and a farewell flag had been run up, our transports began to move on — whither? To the west — to the west — leaving dark volumes of smoke behind! Suddenly clouds gathered in the sky — the rain began to fall, first slowly and then with violence!

Eager brethren! enthusiastic countrymen! Did you expect us soon to return in triumphal procession, when you saw us off; thousands of us starting in good cheer and high spirits?

第二

THE VOYAGE

WITH the nation's Banzai still ringing in our ears, our imaginations flying to stupendous fights over mountains and across rivers, we were being carried far toward the west. Where were we going? Where to land? What was to be the scene of our fighting? All this nobody knew except the colonel as commander of our transportation, and the captains of the transports, to whom secret orders had been given. Even they did not know much at the time of our starting — they were to receive instructions from time to time. Were we going to Chênnam-pu, or to the mouth of the Yalu, or toward Haicheng, or to the siege of Port Arthur? We talked only of our guesses and imaginings. But the place of landing or of fighting did not matter much to us — we were happy at the thought of coming nearer and nearer to the time when we could display all the courage we had, at the word of command from His Majesty and at the beckoning of our regimental flag.

Toward the dusk of the evening on the 21st, we passed through the Strait of Shimonoseki. We

took a last view of our beloved Nippon and felt 第
the pang of separation. 三

"Fare thee well, my land of Yamato! Farewell,
my sweet home!"

That night the Sea of Japan was calm and the
shower of the day had dispersed the clouds. All
was quiet; the thousands of soldiers slept soundly.
Which way did their dreams fly, this first evening
of their expedition — to the east? or to the west?
The gentle waves, the smooth motion of the engines,
an occasional long-drawn breath only added to the
calm of the scene. The next morning we found the
sky well wiped without leaving half a cloud — it
was truly Japan's weather. All the ships at this
moment were hurrying on at full speed off the Isle
of Mutsure, sighting the hills of Tsushima far away
in the distance, when, lo! a hawk[1] descended to the
deck of our transport. The men chased him hither
and thither and rejoiced at this good omen. For
some time the bird remained with us, now perching
on the mast, now flying about over the ship. After
blessing the future of the brave officers and men in
this way, he flew to the next transport to do the same
errand of cheering up their hearts.

Very soon time began to hang heavy on our hands.
To break the monotony of the long voyage, an ap-

[1] The hawk is always the symbol of victory and is associated
in the early legends with Jimmu Tenno's victorious progress
through Yamato.

23

peal to our "hidden accomplishments" was the last but most effective resource. Some would recount their past experiences, others tell ghost stories or jokes, still others recite or sing popular love-episodes, each joining a little group according to his taste or inclination. Every now and then there appeared one bold enough to try the rustic dance of wrestlers, or one clever enough to imitate a professional story-teller, using his knapsack as a book-rest and playing with a fan in his hand, just as a professional reciter would.

Cheers and applause resounded through the small heaven and earth of the steamer, and the performers' faces were full of pride and elation. Others now began to emulate, and from among men piled up like potatoes, story-tellers, conjurers, and performers of various tricks would come forward to amuse the audience.

Proceeding to the front to fight, and to fight never to return, all on this voyage, both men and officers, felt and behaved like one large family, and vied with each other to entertain and beguile the tedious moments, squeezing out all their wit in their tricks and performances and bursting the air and their sides with merry laughter.

Tsushima was then left behind us in mist and haze, and we steered our course northward across the sea, with Korean mountains and peaks still in sight. Our amusements continued day after day,

24

with occasional playing of the piano by clumsy-handed men and shouting and screaming of war-songs on deck. When tired of the game of *go* [1] or of wrestling, we would discuss the plan of campaign and wish that the curtain might be raised at once, so that we could show off our skill on the real stage of the battle-field, not only to astonish the enemy, but to elicit the applause of the world-wide audience.

I remember very well that it was on the 23d of May that our captain asked for our autographs as a memento and family heirloom. I took out a sheet of paper; at its top I sketched the S. S. Kago-shima Maru steering its way, and underneath Colonel Aoki and all the other officers wrote their names. Thirty-seven names this piece of paper contained — only a few of men now surviving! What a valuable and sad memorial it has become! Crippled and useless, I live now as a part and parcel of that memorial, to envy those on the list whose bodies were left in Manchuria and whose honored spirits rest in the Temple of Kudan. [2]

[1] The game of *go*, played with white and black counters on a board ruled into small squares, requires an immense amount of intellectual effort. In this respect it surpasses all games played in America, even chess. It is characteristic of the intellectual activity of the Japanese that this is a favorite game of all classes and all ages.

[2] Kudan, the name of a hill in Tokyo upon which stands the Shokonsha, or "Spirit-Invoking-Temple," wherein are enshrined the spirits of all those who have died for their country. It is one of the religious centres of the New Japan.

On the forenoon of the 24th we were passing near the Elliot Isles, when we saw many lines of smoke floating parallel to the water and sky. It was our combined fleet greeting the approach of our transports. What an inspiring sight, to see our fleet out on the ocean! Presently a cruiser came up to us and continued its course with us. It must have brought some orders for us.

Our landing was near at hand; soon we were to appear on the real stage. And yet we did not know where we were to land; or in what direction we were to march.

All with one accord hoped — Port Arthur!

A DANGEROUS LANDING

WHERE were we to land? This was the question that exercised our minds from the beginning to the end of our voyage. To land at Taku-shan and attack Haicheng and Liao Yang in the north, was one of the suggestions made. To go straight to the Gulf of Pechili and land at Iakao was another. A third suggestion was that we were to land at a certain point on the coast of Liaotung, and then go south to attack the stronghold of Port Arthur. Of course, all the views and opinions advanced were changed according to the direction in which our bows pointed. But at last, when we saw on the chart that we were sailing south of the Elliot Isles, all agreed at once that our destination was some spot leading to Port Arthur. What excitement and joy when we saw the transports and the guard-ships proceeding together toward that spot! After a while we began to notice a dark gray, long, slender piece of land dimly visible through thick mist. That was indeed the Peninsula of Liaotung! the place where, ten years before, so many brave and loyal sons of Yamato had laid their bones,

27

and the field of action on which our own bodies were to be left! Since the previous evening the sky had been dark, the gray mist and clouds opening and shutting from time to time, the wind howling at our mast-heads, and the waves beating against our bows flying like snowflakes and scattering themselves like fallen flowers. Behind us there was only boundless cloud and water. Beyond those clouds was the sky of Nippon! The enthusiastic Banzais of the cheering nation, the sound of rosaries rubbed together in old women's hands, the war-songs coming from the innocent lips of children — all these seemed still to reach our ears, conveyed by the swift winds.

We were to land at a gulf called Yenta-ao, on the eastern coast of the peninsula, to the southwest of Pitsu-wo. This was only a small inlet on the sea of China. There was no good harbor in the vicinity except Talienwan, on the east side of Liaotung Peninsula; but that good harbor was then in possession of the enemy; so we had to risk everything and land on this less desirable spot, from the strategic necessity of the case. The sea and the currents of that neighborhood are both very treacherous; a storm of the least degree would make it extremely difficult, not only to land, but even to stay there at anchor. Moreover, the water is very shallow and a ship of any size must anchor one *ri* [1] away from

---

[1] *Ri*, about two and a half miles.

the shore. When the wind is strong, a ship is sure 第
to drift several miles further to the offing. Such 四
being the case, we can well imagine the difficulty
and anxiety those in charge of our debarkation experienced. Just as mother birds watch over their
young, our convoys were watching us far and near,
to protect our landing from surprise by the enemy.
But the wind that had begun to blow in the morning
became fiercer and fiercer, angry seas and frantic
waves rose in mountains, transports and sampans
were shaken like flying leaves, Chinese junks char-
tered by our government, raising their masts like
forest trees, were being tossed and teazed by the
winds as in the time of the great Mongol invasion
in the Bay of Hakata.[1]

Could we land safely in such a storm? Were we
to face the enemy at once on going ashore? We were
like horses harnessed to a carriage — we did not
know anything about our surroundings. All was
known only to our colonel, in whose hands lay our
lives. We did know, however, that two things were
ahead of us, and they were — landing and marching. After a short wait, our landing was begun in
spite of the risk; evidently the condition of the

[1] The Mongol invasion here referred to is the one of 1274 A.D.,
when Kublai Khan, having made himself master of China and
Korea, undertook the invasion of Japan. His fleet reached the
Bay of Hakata, on the coast of Kyushu, but was dispersed by
a storm after the first battle with the Japanese had driven the
invaders back to their ships.

肉
彈
campaign did not admit delay. Hundreds of sampans, boats, and steam-launches—whence they had come, we did not know—surrounded the transports to carry men and officers away. Tremendous waves, now rising like high mountains and now sinking like deep valleys, seemed to swallow men and boats together. Carrying the flag with due solemnity, I got into the boat with the colonel. Innumerable small boats were to be fastened to steam-launches like beads on a rosary. Rolling and tumbling, these rosaries of boats would whistle their way to the shore. Our regimental flag braved the wind and waves and safely reached its destination. Ah, the first step and the second on this land occupied by the enemy! It seemed as if we had left our Fatherland but yesterday, and now, not in a dream, but in reality, we were treading on the soil of promise!

What an exquisite joy, to plant once more the Imperial Flag of His Illustrious Virtues on the Peninsula of Liaotung, also the soil of Japan, consecrated by the blood of our brothers!

The storm went from bad to worse; it seemed impossible to complete the landing, neither could the men go back to the transports. The only thing possible was to trust to the mercy of winds and waves, jump into the water and struggle for the shore as soon as the boats came near. The experience of my friend Captain Tsukudo is an illustration of the extreme difficulty of landing.

Captain Tsukudo, with over sixty men under his care, was in a boat, which was towed away from the transport by a small launch. His boat rolled in the waves like a ball and was in constant danger of being swallowed in the vortex. The tug cast off her tow and fled for safety. The gigantic *ho* [1] which sweeps through ten thousand miles without rest, even his wings are said to be broken by the waves of the sea. Much less could a small boat stand the force of such waves. It seemed as if the bravest of men had no other choice than being "buried in the stomachs of fishes." Rescue seemed impossible. Heaven's decree they must obey. Death they were ready for, but to die and become refuse of the sea, without having struck one blow at the enemy now close at hand, was something too hard for them to bear. With bloodshot eyes and hair on end, the captain tried in every way to save his men, but alas! they were like a man that falls into an old well in the midst of a lonely meadow, not sinking, yet not able to climb up — the root of the vine that he clings to as a life rope being gnawed by a wild rat!

Captain Tsukudo jumped into the sea and swam toward the shore with all his might; but the waves were too relentless to yield to his impatient and impetuous desire to rescue his men. They swallowed him, vomited him, tossed and hurled him without

[1] *Ho*, a fabulous bird of gigantic size, like the roc of the Arabian Nights.

31

mercy; the brave captain was at last exhausted and fainted away before reaching the shore. Heaven, however, did not give up his case; he was picked up on the beach, and when he recovered consciousness he found himself perfectly naked. Without waiting to dress, he ran to the headquarters of the landing forces, and with frantic gestures asked for help for the men in his boat; he could not weep, for tears were dried up; he could not speak, for his mouth was parched, but he succeeded in getting his men saved.

Another boat loaded with baggage and horses capsized; one of the poor animals swam away toward the offing. The soldier in charge of the horse also swam to catch the animal. Before he reached it, the steed went down and soon afterward the faithful man also disappeared in the billows. Poor, brave soul! his love of his four-legged charge was stronger even than that of the stork who cries after its young in the lonesome night. Though he did not face the enemy's bullets, he died a pioneer's death on the battle-field of duty.

Was the Canaan of our hopes the country that we had pictured to ourselves? Contrary to our expectations, it did not look at all like a place our brethren had bought with their blood ten years before. It was simply a desolate wilderness, a deserted sand-plain, a boundless expanse of rolling country, a monotonous insipid canvas, with dark red and light gray all over. Compared with the detailed, variegated picture of Japan that we had been accustomed to, what a sense of untouched and unfinished carelessness! What a change of scene to see hundreds of natives swarm to the spot of our landing, with horses and wagons, to get their job! Were they men or animals? With ill-favored faces, they would whisper to each other and pass on. As knavish fellows they deserve anything but love, but as subjects of an ill-governed empire they certainly deserve pity. At first they dreaded the Japanese; they stared at us from a distance, but did not come near us; probably because they had been robbed of their possessions by the Russians, and their wives and daughters had been insulted by them. The Japanese army, from the very first, was extremely careful to be just and kind to the natives and encouraged them to pursue their daily work in peace. Consequently they soon began to be friendly with us and to welcome us eagerly. However, they are a race of men who would risk even their lives to make money, and would live in a pig-pen with ten thousand pieces of gold in their pockets. How our army suffered from the treachery of these money-grubbers will be told later on.

"Ata, ata! Wo, wo!"

This strange cry we constantly heard at the front — it is the natives' way of driving horses and cows. Their skill in managing cattle and horses is far

33

beyond ours. We could not help being struck with the manner in which the animals obeyed their orders; they would go to right or left at the sound of these signals, and would move as one's own limbs without the slightest use of whips. The relation between these natives and their cattle and horses is like that between well-disciplined soldiers and their commanders; not the fear of whip and scolding, but a voluntary respect and submission, is the secret of military discipline and success. The fact that the Russian soldiers were lacking in this important factor became clear later by the testimony of the captives.

After some companies of our division had landed with much ado, the storm grew worse and the landing was suspended. The colonel, an aide-de-camp, the interpreter, the chaplain, and myself, accompanied by a handful of guards, crossed the wilderness and wended our way toward Wangchia-tun, fixed as our stopping-place for that night. We busied ourselves with the map and the compass, while the interpreter asked question after question of the natives. I consulted a Chinese-Japanese conversation book, and asked them in broken words, "Russian soldiers, have they come?" to which they replied, "To Port Arthur they have fled." We were of course disappointed not to encounter the long-looked-for antagonists at once!

Seven *ri*'s journey through a sand plain brought

34

us to the willow-covered village Wangchia-tun in the rainy and windy evening, when strange birds were hastening to their roosts.

Stupid-looking old men and dirty-faced boys gathered round us like ants and looked at us with curiosity. Long pipes were sticking out from the mouths of the older men; they seemed utterly unconcerned or ignorant of the great trouble in their own country. The filth and dirt of the houses and their occupants were beyond description; we newcomers to the place had to hold our noses against the fearful smells. Military camp though it was in name, we only found shelter under the eaves of the houses, with penetrating smells attacking us from below, and surrounded by large and small Chinese highly scented with garlic! Before our hungry stomachs could welcome the toasted rice-balls, our olfactory nerves would rebel against the feast.

We who had succeeded in landing spent our first night in Liaotung in this condition. The spirits of the deceased comrades of ten years before must have welcomed us with outstretched arms and told us what they expected of us. Under tents, half exposed to the cold and wet, the men slept the good sleep of the innocent on millet straw, and an occasional smile came to their unconscious lips. What were they dreaming of? Some there were who sat by the smoky fire of millet straw all the night through, buried in deep thought and munching the remnant of their parting gifts with their lunch boxes hanging from the stone wall.

The day was about to dawn, when suddenly thunder and lightning arose in the western sky. Not lightning, but flames of fire; not thunder, but roar of cannon! Furious winds added to the dreariness of the scene; the sky was the color of blood.

The great battle of Nanshan! We could not keep still from fullness of joy and excitement.

第
五

THE VALUE OF PORT ARTHUR

THAT glorious January 2, of the thirty-eighth year of Meiji, will never be forgotten to the end of time. That happy day of the victorious New Year was doubly crowned by the birth of an Imperial grandson and by the capitulation of Port Arthur! There has never been a New Year in all our history so auspicious and so memorable!

The fall of Port Arthur was an event that marked an epoch in the history of the world! Do not forget, however, that this result was achieved only through the shedding of rivers of blood. General Kuropatkin had boasted of the invincible strength of the fortress and had said that it could live out over a year against the fiercest attacks imaginable. But the incessant, indefatigable rain of bullets and shells upon the place by the invading army obliged the Russians to surrender in less than two hundred and fifty days. Between the first battle at Nanshan and the final capitulation of Stoessel, the bodies of our soldiers became hills and their blood rivulets. Spectators often doubted our success. But the spirit of Yamato, as firm as the iron

37

肉
弾

of a hundred times beating and as beautiful as the cherries blooming on ten thousand boughs — that *tamashii*[1] proved too powerful for the completest of mechanical defense. At the same time, we cannot but admire the stubborn courage with which the Russian generals and soldiers defended their posts under circumstances of extreme difficulty and suffering. We fully endorse the remark of a foreign critic: "Well attacked and well defended!"

Port Arthur had been attracting the keen attention of the whole world ever since the Japan-China war. Russia had spent nearly ten years and hundreds of millions of yen[2] in fortifying the place. It had been considered of such strategic importance that its fall would mark the practical termination of the Russo-Japanese struggle, just as the fall of Plevna decided the fate of the Russo-Turkish war. The fortress of Port Arthur embraces within its arms its town and harbor — innumerable hills of from two to five hundred metres in height form a natural protection to the place. To these natural advantages was added the world-famous skill of the Russians in fortification. Every hill, every eminence had every variety of fortification, with countless cannon, machine-guns, and rifles,

[1] *Tamashii*, spirit, the same word that in composition with Yamato becomes *damashii*.

[2] Yen, the monetary unit, equal to one hundred sen, or fifty cents.

so that an attack either from the front or from the side could easily be met. Each spot was made still more unapproachable by ground-mines, pitfalls, wire-entanglements, etc. There was hardly any space where even an ant could get in unmolested. It was surely impregnable. On the other hand, our position was extremely disadvantageous. We had to climb a steep hill, or go down into a deep valley, or up an exposed slope to attack any Russian fort. The position of the whole place was such that it was as easy to defend as it was difficult to attack. Moreover, the Russians had on the spot enough provisions and ammunition to withstand a longer siege, without relying upon supplies from outside.

But there is no single instance in history of any fort that has withstood siege permanently; sooner or later it must either capitulate or else lose all its men and fall. The same will also be the case in the future. The only question is whether a fort will fall as easily as a castle of *amê*.[1] Sebastopol withstood the allied armies of England and France for more than three hundred and twenty days, but eventually fell after the docks had been destroyed, the forts blown up, and the town utterly demolished. At *Kars* the gallant General Williams, with only three months' provision and three days' ammunition, supported by the Turkish soldiers, withstood for seven months the Russian army of fifty thou-

[1] *Amê*, candy made from wheat gluten.

sand men; but it fell at last. The Russian General Muravieff admired the hero of *Kars* and sent him this message:—

"All the world and future generations will marvel at your valor and discipline. Let us have the glory of consulting together about the way of satisfying the requirements of war, without doing harm to the cause of humanity."

Paris resisted the Prussian siege for one hundred and thirty-two days before surrendering. These are only a few remarkable examples in history; but all besieged places have fallen sooner or later. The only purpose a fort can serve is to resist the besiegers as long as possible, so as to hinder the general plan of the enemy. This principle applied to Port Arthur; it had to detain as many as possible of the Japanese in the south, for as many days as possible, in order to let Kuropatkin develop his plan in North Manchuria without hindrance. For this great object, General Stoessel held fast to the marvelously fortified place and tried his best to keep off the besieging army. Supposing that Port Arthur had not fallen before the great battle of Moukden, what would it have meant to our general plan of campaign? This supposition will make the true value of Port Arthur clear to every mind. Therefore they tried to hold it, and we endeavored to take it; a desperate defense on one side and a desperate attack on the other. General Nogi bought the fortress at a tremendous price — the sacrifice of tens of thousands of lives; but once in our possession, its value became greater than ever.

That such an invincible and unapproachable place was taken in eight months tells how fierce was the struggle. The siege of Port Arthur was one of the bloodiest contests that the world has known. In modern history, the siege of Plevna had until then been considered the most sanguinary. The great but unfortunate artist, Vereshtchagin, who went to the bottom of the sea outside Port Arthur with Admiral Makaroff, painted for posterity the scenes of Plevna. If he had survived to see the last of Port Arthur, he must have portrayed a scene even more bloody. Mr. George Kennan, the war-correspondent of the "Outlook," described this siege as representing the shriek of the lowest hell on this earthly abode of ours. And these horrible scenes were necessitated by the strategic value of Port Arthur itself.

How was Port Arthur besieged and attacked? The answer to this question is the centre and object of my little sketch; hence this brief explanation of its value.

The night of our landing at Liaotung, we heard the din of battle arising from Nanshan, the only entrance to Port Arthur. Let us now return to that battle.

THE BATTLE OF NANSHAN

THE thunder and lightning in the direction of Nanshan became fiercer and fiercer as time went on. How was it being fought? With what courage and perseverance were our comrades acquitting themselves? Was the place already occupied, or were they still struggling on? We must hurry forward to take part in this our first battle; it was an opportunity too great for us to miss. How soon should we be ordered to march? We were thus impatient and fidgeting, our minds racing toward Nanshan. But, on the other hand, we did not know whether the battalions to follow us had accomplished their landing in safety or not. The messenger sent for news had not come back after a day and night. The colonel had only five hundred men in hand. What a slender force! Would our commander venture out with this handful of men? His anxious face told us that he could not lead us at once into the fight. Were we merely to watch it from a distance, as if it were a fire on the other side of a river, without offering to help? We began to be disappointed. Of course the prospect of the war was long—the curtain had just risen; this Nanshan could not be the last act. But it was tantalizing to be on the spot and yet not to encounter the enemy, to hear the din of battle and yet not be able to join!

All things come to him who waits. We received the following orders: —

"Proceed without delay to join the Second Army under General Oku at Nanshan."

This was proclaimed by our colonel, who was full of joy and eagerness — his voice rang with energy and enthusiasm. Both men and officers welcomed the news as they would glad tidings from heaven. They were more than ready to start. March! tear on! We spread our legs as wide as possible. We kicked and spurned village after village, field after field. We did not think of how many miles we ran. With the enemy's visage lurking before our eyes, we did not feel any pain or fatigue; the drops of perspiration mixed with dust formed a mask over our faces — but what did it matter? Our water bottles were emptied ere long, our throats were dry and parched, we were almost suffocating, but not a single man was out of rank. We all looked toward the supposed post of the enemy, and ran forward. The sound of roaring cannon made us forget fatigue, difficulty, and pain.

"Is Nanshan still holding out?"

"They're just in the thick of the fight — hurry on, men!"

肉
弾

Such conversations were frequently heard between the coolies coming back from Nanshan and the men now marching to it. It sounds foolish, but we all wished that Nanshan would not yield before our arrival. Perhaps we were conceited enough to think that, without the help of us fresh men, our comrades would be too exhausted to occupy the place. When we saw on our way two or three captured officers being escorted to our headquarters, we were half happy to have a first sight of the defeated enemy and half afraid lest Nanshan had already been taken!

I wish to say in passing that in the army a sharp line is drawn between the things that may be granted to the soldiers when possible and those that must not be allowed under any circumstances. This is particularly the case in time of a march. In a march for practice, or in a march in time of war, but not for an actual engagement, as much rest and as ample a supply of provisions are allowed as possible. But when we march to a fight, we go on even without food or water, or in spite of a heavy storm. Each soldier carries a knapsack about ten *kwan* [1] in weight, and has only one bottleful of water to drink. When he has emptied it, he cannot get one drop more. Day after day, he rests and sleeps in a field-encampment; in pouring rain or howling storm, he is not allowed to take shelter even under the

[1] *Kwan*, a little over eight and a quarter pounds.

44

eaves of a house. Exhaustion or pain is no reason for an exception. He has no time to wipe the perspiration from his face, which soon becomes white with dried-up salt. Panting and suffocating, he struggles on. It seems cruelty to subject men to this ordeal, but they must sacrifice everything to duty. Even one single soldier must not be missing, even one single rifle must not be lacking from the skirmish line. And after such a hard march, they engage in a severe fight at once; so, therefore, the success or failure of the battle is practically settled during the march. Hence the great importance of training men in time of peace in waterless marches, night marches, and quick marches. This practice may seem needlessly inflicted hardship, but its true value is made clear when it comes to a real fight.

To return to our story, we pressed on in great enthusiasm or rather in a state of frenzy, thinking all the while of the first battle at Nanshan. When we came near our destination, we saw cone-shaped tents nestling under the trees or on the sides of the hills. They were our field-hospitals. The large number of these tents made us very anxious about the issue of the struggle. Stretcher after stretcher would bring fresh patients and hurry back to the line of battle to fetch more. The wounded who could walk accompanied the stretchers on foot in large numbers and panting all the way. Both those on foot and those on stretchers were covered with

第六

45

blood and mud, which told more eloquently than words the story of their valiant fight and hard struggle. Their white bandages, stained with red, covered wounds of honor; the drops of blood falling through the stretchers seemed to hallow the ground. They impressed us with an inexpressible dignity — we could not help sighing with reverence and gratitude.

Just at this moment, the aide-de-camp who had gone forward to receive instructions came back and reported that Nanshan had fallen, and that all the reserves were to lodge in the neighborhood of Chungchia-tun to await further orders. What a disappointment! From the commander down to the grooms all felt dispirited and disheartened — stroked their hard-strained arms and stamped on the ground with regret. It is true, this early fall of Nanshan, which the enemy had considered the key to Port Arthur, would be a great advantage to our future plan of campaign. We ought to have rejoiced over the news, and we did of course rejoice; but at the same time you cannot blame us for being thus disappointed when you think how we had hurried and pressed on from the point of our landing, without stopping to recover our breath, only to learn at our destination that the object of our efforts had been attained by other people.

Only one more hill in front of us! Beyond it were blood-streams and corpse-hills. When we reached this spot the deafening cannon roar suddenly ceased, the mountains and valleys recovered their ancient silence. The only thing we saw was the continuous sending back of the wounded. Whenever we met them, we comforted them and thanked them for their work. We had a rest at the bottom of the hill, where a groom, who had been in the battle, re-counted to us the story with great pride. Shaking his head and flourishing his arms, he talked like a professional story-teller — his story was a great excitement for us then. He showed us a water bottle that had belonged to a Russian soldier. Alto-gether he talked as if he had vanquished the enemy all by himself. We who had not yet loaded our guns, we who had not yet unsheathed our swords, felt shamefaced and crestfallen; even this non-combatant groom seemed like a hero to us. We praised him, and piled question after question on him, and eagerly devoured his triumphant ac-counts.

We, all the reserves under the direct command of General Oku, Commander-in-chief of the Second Army, were ordered to spend the night at Chung-chia-tun. We had to go back a *ri* and a half over the same road to that place. How lacking in spirit was that backward march! Both men and horses hung their heads and walked on dejectedly. The yellow dust rising from the ground made us look like dumplings covered with yellow bean-flour. In our

47

forced march by day and night, we had thought only of Nanshan and had not felt any pain in our legs. Everything was reversed on our return! Even in a manœuvre in time of peace, the sound of cannon and rifles makes us forget the pain in our feet and the exhaustion of our bodies, changes our walking into running, and incites us to assault the enemy with a frantic zeal; but once we begin to retrace our steps, our feet grow heavy at once, every rut and every pebble tries our temper, and we are entirely without energy or spirit. This may come from the Japanese characteristic that thinks only of going forward and not at all of retreating. The Russian soldiers are masterly in retreat, whilst the Japanese are very unskilled in it. But once they begin to advance, the Japanese are never defeated by the Russians. We have inherited a temperament which knows no retreating even before sure death, and that inheritance has been made stronger by discipline. Our constant victory over the fierce enemy must largely be due to this characteristic of ours.

At last we reached Chungchia-tun. It was a desolate village with a small stream running through it. The moon looked dismal that night and the stars were few. Nature seemed to sympathize with the disappointed, worn-out men and officers, sleeping on millet straw and mourning over those who had died in the battle of that day. Here and there we saw men unable to go to sleep till late at night —

48

their hearts must have been full of new emotions. The cuckoo [1] hurrying through the sky, with one brief note or two — a few bars of a *biwa*-song [2] crooned by a sleepless man — Ah, what a lonesome, touching evening it was!

Thus I failed to take part in the battle of Nanshan, and I have no right to recount the story of that severe struggle, although the title of this chapter may suggest a full recital. The only thing I can do is to tell you in the next chapter what I saw on the scene of the battle immediately after its actual occurrence. This will be followed up later by my own story of the siege of Port Arthur. Before concluding this chapter, however, I wish to introduce a brave soldier to my readers.

When we were starting from Wangchia-tun we dispatched a bicycle orderly, Buichi Kusunoki by name, to our place of landing, Yenta-ao, to establish communication between ourselves and those who landed after we did. This man was known to be specially fitted to fulfill such a duty; his perseverance and undaunted courage had always made him successful. Consequently, when we started from Japan, he was singled out from his company as an orderly attached to the headquarters of our regi-

[1] In Japanese poetry the cuckoo's rare cry in the moonlight is treated as particularly sad and dismal.

[2] A species of epic, or heroic ballad, sung to the accompaniment of the lute, or *biwa*, which has always been the music of the Japanese soldier.

肉
弾

ment. So, naturally, this first important duty after our landing devolved upon Kusunoki. Late in the afternoon, he started for Yenta-ao on his machine. We had come to Wangchia-tun through pathless plains—he could not expect to go back to Yenta-ao without great difficulty. In a strange land, not knowing anything of the place or the language, he went on with the pole-star as his only guide. His duty was very important. If he had reached his destination even one hour later, much time would have been lost in the movement of the other detachments. Of course he did not know that Nanshan was to fall without our help. He only knew that our whole regiment of reserves must be near Nanshan, so that we could join the battle-line at a moment's notice. This Kusunoki was the sole means of communication by which the two separate parts of our regiment could be brought together. On starting, he was carefully told of the tremendous responsibility he was to undertake. But eight or nine *ri*'s journey in the pathless wilderness of Liaotung in pitch darkness was not an easy task. His bicycle, instead of being a help, was a burden to him; he had to carry it on his back and run. He went astray and could not find the right place all night. Toward daybreak he hoped to be able to find out where he was, but all in vain! With nothing to eat or drink, he struggled on without knowing whither he was going, but praying that he might chance to reach the right place.

50

With his mind in a great hurry, he crept on all fours, resting every now and then, for his legs would carry him no further with his machine on his back. Fortunately, however, he came across a sentinel, who showed him the right way and gave him something to eat. He was thus enabled to accomplish his object in time, — though delayed. The orderly, and the aide-de-camp as well, bears a responsibility much greater than that of an ordinary soldier. The commander must rely upon them if he would move tens of thousands of men as easily as he moves his own fingers. The success or failure of a whole army often depends upon the efficiency of the aide-de-camp. Therefore he must possess the four important qualities of courage, perseverance, judgment, and prompt decision. And this Buichi Kusunoki was a true aide-de-camp, with bravery and faithfulness worthy of our profound respect.

NANSHAN AFTER THE BATTLE

NANSHAN guards Chin-chou at the entrance to the Liaotung Peninsula. Though its hills are not steep or rugged, they go far back in great waves. The place is convenient for defensive purposes, but it is inferior in this respect to Nankwanling, farther back. In the China-Japan War, the Chinese resisted us for a while at this Nankwanling. The reason why the Russians preferred to fortify Nanshan rather than Nankwanling was because the former was near Dalny, their only non-freezing port. They had chosen a spot on the opposite shore from Lin Shin Ton, the railway terminus at the head of Talie Bay, and had built there the large city of Dalny, making it their only commercial port in Liaotung and the starting-point of the Eastern China Railway. In order to protect this port, they had chosen Nanshan at its back and built there a fortification of a semi-permanent character. For ten years they had been spending hundreds of millions in building this city and fortifying Port Arthur, and at the same time in strengthening this important outpost of Nanshan. We were told by

a captured Russian staff-officer that the Russians
had believed that Nanshan could stand the fiercest
attacks of the Japanese for more than half a year.
However, when our second army began to attack
the place, they set at naught every difficulty, did
not grudge any amount of sacrifice, and precipitated
themselves upon the enemy so violently that Chin-
chou, Nanshan, and Dalny were all occupied in one
single night and day (May 26). You can well imagine how desperate was this struggle. Even in the
China-Japan War, the taking of Nankwanling and
the occupation of Port Arthur were not quite as easy
as to twist a baby's arm. But one Japanese officer,
who fought on both occasions, said to us, when he
examined the elaborate defenses of Nanshan, that
the battle of ten years before had only been a
sham fight in comparison. We had to sacrifice over
four thousand men killed and wounded in order to
take this stronghold. The scene after the battle
presented a terrible sight. True it is that this battle
was very mild compared with the general assault on
Port Arthur, but at Nanshan I saw for the first time
in my life the shocking scenes after a furious fight.

We managed somehow to pass the night of the
26th at Chungchia-tun, and on the next morning
we received instructions to go out and lodge at
Yenchia-tun, a village at the foot of Nanshan.
The fifth and sixth companies of our regiment were
ordered to guard Nanshan.

53

As soon as we reached the top of the steep hill that I have already mentioned, an extensive rolling country was before our eyes. At its right was Chinchou, while on the left the steep Fahoshangshan reared its head. This was the site of the fierce battle of yesterday. The place was full of reminders of cannon roar and war-cries; we could not stand the sight. Horrible is the only word that describes the scene.

From a hill in front of us we saw white smoke rising and spreading a strange odor far and wide; that was the cremation of our brave dead, the altar on which the sacrifice to the country was being burned. Hundreds of patriotic souls must have risen to heaven enveloped in that smoke. We took off our caps and bowed to them. While the mothers at home were peacefully reeling thread and thinking of their beloved sons at the front, while the wives, with their babies on their backs, were sewing and thinking of their dear husbands, these sons and husbands were being crushed to pieces and turned into volumes of smoke.

It is not pleasant to see even a piece of a blood-stained bandage. It is shocking to see dead bodies piled up in this valley or near that rock, dyed with dark purple blood, their faces blue, their eyelids swollen, their hair clotted with blood and dust, their white teeth biting their lips, the red of their uniforms alone remaining unchanged. I could not

54

help shuddering at the sight and thinking that I myself might soon become like that. No one dared to go near and look carefully at those corpses. We only pointed to them from a distance in horror and disgust. Everywhere were scattered blood-covered gaiters, pieces of uniform and underwear, caps, and so on; everywhere were loathsome smells and ghastly sights. Innumerable powder-boxes and empty cartridges, piled up near the skirmish-trenches, told us plainly how desperately the enemy had fired upon the invading army. Wherever we saw the enemy's dead left on the field, we could not help sympathizing with them. They were enemies, but they also fought for their own country. We buried them carefully, but the defeated heroes of the battle had no names that we could hand down to posterity. At home their parents, their wives, and their children must have been anxiously waiting for their safe return, not knowing, in most cases, when, where, or how their beloved ones had been killed. Almost all of them had a cross on the chest, or an ikon in hand. Let us hope that they passed away with God's blessing and guidance. The killed and wounded of a defeated army deserve the greatest pity. Of course they are entitled to equal and humane treatment by the enemy, according to the International Red Cross regulations. But defeat we must avoid by all means. Added to the ignominy of defeat, the wounded must have the sorrow of separating from their comrades

55

和living or dying among perfect strangers, with whom they cannot even converse. The case of the killed is still sadder. Some had cards of identification, so that their numbers would eventually tell their names. As far as we could, we informed the enemy of those numbers; but there were many instances where there was no means of identification. Their names are buried in eternal obscurity.

Arrangements were made for our temporary lodgment at Yenchia-tun. When I reached the native house assigned for us that evening, I heard next door the piteous groanings of human beings. I hastened to the spot to see the tortures of hell itself. Fifteen or sixteen Japanese, and one Russian, all seriously wounded, were lying in the yard, heaped one above another, and writhing in an agony of pain. The first one who noticed my coming put his hands together in supplication and begged me for help. What need of his begging? To help is our privilege. I could not imagine why these poor comrades should have been left alone in such a condition. If we had known earlier, perhaps better assistance could have been given. With tears of sympathy I called in surgeons and helped in relieving their suffering. While the surgeons were attending to their wounds they would repeat: "I shall never forget your goodness; I am grateful to you." These words were squeezed out of the bottom of their hearts, and their eyes were full of tears. On inquiry we learned that for two

56

days they had not had a single grain of rice, or a single drop of water. They were all very severely wounded, with broken legs, shattered arms, or bullet wounds in head or chest. Some there were who could not live more than half an hour longer; even these were taking each other's hands or stroking each other in sympathy and to comfort. How sad! How pitiful! How boundless must be our sadness and pity when we think that there were over four thousand killed and wounded on our side alone, and that it was impossible to give them the attention they needed! In a short time two of the men began to lose color, and breathe faintly. I ran to their side and watched. Their eyes gradually closed and their lips ceased to quiver. One comrade near by told me that one of these two had left an old mother at home alone.

One of the most pitiful of sights is, perhaps, the dead or wounded war-horses. They had crossed the seas to run and gallop in a strange land among flying bullets and the roar of cannon. They seemed to think that this was the time to return their masters' kindness in keeping them comfortable so long. With their masters on their backs they would run about so cheerfully and gallantly on the battle-field! The pack-horses also seemed proud and anxious to show their long-practiced ability in bearing heavy burdens or drawing heavy carts, without complaining of their untold sufferings. Their usefulness in war

第七

is beyond description. The successful issue of a battle is due first to the efforts of the brave men and officers, but we must not forget what we owe to the help of our faithful animals. And yet they are so modest of their merits; are contented with coarse fodder and muddy water; do not grumble at continual exposure to rain and snow, and think their master's caress the best comfort they can have. Their manner of performing their important duties is almost equal to that of soldiers. But they are speechless; they cannot tell of wound or pain. Sometimes they cannot get medicine, or even a comforting pat. They writhe in agony and die unnoticed, with a sad neigh of farewell. Their bodies are not buried, but are left in the field for wolves and crows to feed upon, their big strong bones to be bleached in the wild storms of the wilderness. These loyal horses also are heroes who die a horrible death in the performance of duty; their memory ought to be held in respect and gratitude. My teacher, the Rev. Kwatsurin Nakabayashi,[1] accompanied our army during the war as a volunteer nurse. While taking care of the wounded at the front, he collected fragments of shells to use in erecting an image of Bato-Kwanon[2]

[1] A Buddhist priest.

[2] Kwanon is the Buddhist Goddess of Mercy. Bato-Kwanon, or the Horse-headed Kwanon, is the special patroness of horses. In the country districts one may see rude images of Bato-Kwanon set up by the roadside, to which horses are brought and offerings made by their masters in their behalf.

58

to comfort the spirits of the horses that died in the war. This plan of his has already been carried out. Another Buddhist by the name of Doami has been urging an International Red Cross Treaty for horses such as there is now for men. Without such a provision he says we cannot claim to be true to the principles of humanity. Our talk of love and kindness to animals will be an empty sound. He is said to be agitating the introduction of such a proposition at the next Hague Conference. Of course there are veterinary surgeons in the army, but no one can expect them to be able to bestow all necessary care on the unfortunate animals. To supply this deficiency and protect animals as best we can, a Red Cross for horses is a proposal worthy of serious attention.

I climbed Nanshan to inspect the arrangements of the enemy's position there. Everything was almost ideal in their plan of defense, everything quite worthy of a great military power. Besides the wire-entanglements, pitfalls, ground-mines, strong lines of trenches went round and round the mountain, embrasure holes for machine guns were seen everywhere, a large number of heavy guns thrust out their muzzles from many a fort. As the place was fortified in a semi-permanent style, there were barracks and storehouses, and the latter were filled with all kinds of winter clothing. There was a railway and also a battery. When I entered a building used as the headquarters of the commander, I was

第七

astonished to find how luxuriously and comfortably he had lived there. His rooms were beautifully furnished, hardly reminding one of camp life. What was most curious, night garments and toilet articles of a feminine nature as well as children's clothes were scattered here and there.

From this spot I looked through field-glasses far to the eastern seacoast, where were countless men and horses lying on the beach washed by the gray waves. They were the remains of the Cavalry Brigade of the enemy, who had been stationed about Laohu-shan to defend the right flank of their lines. Our Fourth Division surprised them from behind, from the west coast; they had no way of retreat, were driven into the sea, and thus were almost all drowned. This defeat was self-inflicted, in so far as they had relied too much upon the strength of their position and thus lost the opportunity for a timely retreat.

Half-way up the mountain we saw a damaged search-light and a pile of rockets. These were the things that often impeded our attempts at coming near the enemy under cover of night. The search-light had been damaged by our men in revenge after the occupation of the place, because they had been so severely harassed by the machine.

The scene before my eyes filled my heart with grief and sorrow. Hour after hour the wooden posts to mark the burial-places of the dead increased in number. On my trip of observation from Nanshan to Chin-chou I noticed a mound of loose earth, with a bamboo stick planted on it. I stepped on the mound to see what it was. I was shocked to discover a dead Russian underneath. It was my first experience of stepping on a corpse, and I cannot forget the horror I felt. At that time I had not yet tasted a fight and therefore could not help shuddering at its tragic and sinful effects. It is almost curious to think of it now, for the oftener flying bullets are encountered the less sensitive we become to the horrors of war. What is shocking and sickening becomes a matter of indifference. Familiarity takes off the edge of sensibility. If we should continue to be so shocked and disgusted we could not survive the strain.

For sixteen hours our army persevered, braved the cross-firing of the enemy, and finally captured Nanshan after several assaults with a large sacrifice of precious lives. We thus acquired the key to the whole peninsula of Chin-chou, cut off the communication of the enemy, were enabled to begin the clearing of Talien Bay unmolested, and also to make all necessary preparations for the general attack on Port Arthur. Our victory at Nanshan was a record-breaking event in the annals of warfare. And this signal success was won, not through the power of powder and gun, but primarily through the courage and perseverance of our men. During the battle, when the third assault failed of success, the commander, General Oku, cried in a voice of thunder,

第七

"What sort of a thing is Yamato-damashi?" Whereupon the whole army gained fresh strength, drew one long breath, and took the place by storm. Sir Claude MacDonald said that the secret of Japan's unbroken record of success in this war was in the "men behind the guns." This battle of Nanshan was a demonstration of their quality.

DIGGING AND SCOUTING

IT was on the 28th of May that we went to Chang-chia-tun from Yenchia-tun to take the place of the defense corps of the Third Division. After Nan-shan our division was separated from the Second Army under Oku, and attached to the newly organized Third Army for the siege of Port Arthur. It was not a long march from Yenchia-tun to Chang-chia-tun, but whenever I think about marching I cannot help remembering this particular occasion. Round about Port Arthur the ground is covered with rocks and pebbles; all the other places on the peninsula are covered with earth like rice bran or ashes, which fills the mouth, eyes, and nose. Swift winds stirred up clouds of dust, filling the throat and threatening to swallow the long snake-like line of marching men. Often we could not see an inch ahead and our line of men was in danger of disconnection. Even the cooked rice in our lunch boxes was filled with the dust. On other occasions we had marched ten or twenty *ri*'s without resting day or night, had covered sometimes a distance of more than ten *ri*'s on the double-quick, had made a forced

63

肉 march without a drop of drinking water, or had
弾 marched in pitch darkness; but all our previous experiences of this kind were nothing compared with
the hardships of this dust-covered march. If this is
the price for the honor of taking part in a real war,
we have certainly paid it. Toil and hardship of
course we were ready for, but while our minds were
prepared for bayonets and bullets, at first we felt it
a torture to fight with Nature herself, to cross the
wilderness, climb the mountains, fight with rain
and wind, with heat and cold, and sleep on the beds
of grass. But very soon we began to philosophize,
and to think that this was also an important part of
our warfare, and this idea made us take kindly to
the fight with the elements and with Nature. Eventually we learned to enjoy sleeping in the spacious
mansion of millet fields, or in rock-built castles,
viewing the moon and listening in our beds to the
singing of insects.

Marching without a halt, we reached Chang-
chia-tun and took the place of the Third Division
men. When we saw these men for the first time,
we felt ashamed of our own inexperience and wished
to sneak out of their sight. They seemed to us
crowned with glory for their great achievement at
Nanshan, and we felt like country people who had
missed the train, looking at the trail of smoke with
mouths wide open in disappointment. We envied
them, picturing to ourselves their clothes torn and

bloodstained and their skins covered with fresh wounds of honor. We looked up to them with love and reverence, admiring their dust-covered caps and bloodstained gaiters. Their very countenances, their very demeanor, seemed to recount eloquently their glorious exploits.

The right centre of our line of defense was an eminence facing the enemy's front. But our whole line covered a distance of twenty-five kilometres from Antsu-shan at one end to Taitzu-shan at the other, with the pass of Mantutsu in the middle. Just north of this pass is the village of Lichia-tun, and our own battalion occupied a line extending from this village at its right to the village of Yuchia-tun the other side of the river, beyond which lay a range of hills. There we raised strong works, diligently sought our enemy, and busily engaged ourselves in preparations for defense and attack. In the meantime General Nogi and his staff landed at Yenta-ao and reached Peh-Paotsu-yai, a village about three *ri*'s to the northwest of Dalny. With his arrival the organization of the Third Army was completed. How eagerly, then, did we wait for the first chance of fighting!

The enemy, though defeated at Nanshan, had of course been reluctant to give up Dalny; but they had been obliged to run for their lives, and they and their wives and children escaped toward the bottom of the bag, that is, Port Arthur, burning down the village of Sanshihli-pu on their way thither. They had fortified a strong line, connecting the hills, Pantu, Lwanni-chiao, Waitu, Shwangting, etc. The distance between the Russian and Japanese lines was between three and five thousand metres. This much of the enemy's condition and position we ascertained through the hard work of scouts and scouting parties.

As soon as we were stationed on the line of defense, we began on the very first day to work with pickaxes and shovels. A special spot was assigned to each cavalry battalion and infantry company, and each group of men, in its own place, hurried day and night, digging trenches for skirmishers. The officers acted as "bosses," the non-commissioned officers as foremen, and the men themselves as coolies, —all were engaged in digging earth. All the while scouts, both officers and non-commissioned officers, were being dispatched to find out the enemy's movements. No alarm had come yet; the engineering work made daily progress. The trenches for skirmishers and bomb-proofs for the cavalry, forming the first line of defense, grew steadily, their breastworks strengthened by sand-bags the sacking for which had been brought from Dalny. A simple kind of wire-entanglement was also put up, a good road was made, short cuts connecting different bodies of men were laid out like cobwebs; thus our defenses assumed almost a half-permanent character. The soldiers either utilized village dwellings, or pitched tents in the yards or under the trees. When all these necessary preparations were fairly complete, more scouts and scouting parties began to go off to find out the movements and whereabouts of the enemy.

At a military review or manœuvres in time of peace, the men look gay and comfortable, but on the real battle-field they have to try a true life-and-death match with the enemy. In the readiness and morale of the men while on the outposts lies the outcome of the actual encounter. Therefore men on the line of defense cannot sleep at ease at night, or kindle fires to warm themselves. The night is the time when they must be most vigilant and wide-awake. The patrols on the picket line and the scouts far in front must try to take in everything. However tired they may be from their day's work, at night they must not allow even a singing insect or a flying bird to pass unnoticed. Holding their breath and keeping their heads cool, they must use their sight and hearing for the whole army behind them, with the utmost vigilance. When people talk of war, they usually forget the toil and responsibility of the men on the picket line, they talk only of their behavior on the field of battle. Because this duty was neglected, three regiments of the English army in the War of Independence, 1777, were annihilated by the Americans through the fault of one single sentinel.

"Halt! Halt! Who goes there?"

The sentinel's cry adds to the loneliness of an anxious night. One or two shots suddenly sound through the silent darkness; it is probable that the enemy's pickets have been discovered. Quiet prevails once more; the night is far advanced. A bank of dark clouds starts from the north, spreads quickly and covers the whole sky with an inky color, and the rain begins to fall drop by drop. This experience on the picket line, keeping a sharp eye on the enemy all the time, continued for about thirty days.

By the time our line of defense was in proper order, the enemy began to show their heads. Every night there was the report of rifles near our line of patrols.

"Captain, five or six of the enemy's infantry scouts appeared, and then suddenly disappeared, in a valley five or six hundred metres ahead." Such a report was repeated over and over again in the course of one day and night. Soon we began to try various contrivances to capture the enemy's scouts on our line of patrol. One of them was this: about twenty *ken*[1] away from our line a piece of rope was stretched, to that rope another piece was fastened, one end of it leading to the spot where our patrol was standing. The idea was that if the enemy walked against the first rope the second would com-

[1] The *ken* measures about six feet.

68

municate the vibration to the patrol man. Once when the signal came, and the men hurried to capture the enemy, no human being was in sight, but a large black dog stood barking and snarling at them.

第
九

THE FIRST CAPTIVES

OUR scouts were gradually increased in number; not only from the troops on the first line, but also from the reserves at the rear, scouts were dispatched one after another. Almost always they were successful. They either came across a small body of the enemy and dispersed them, or else they came back with the report of a place where a larger force was stationed. Such a success was always welcome to the commander of the brigade or of the regiment. Because we had not yet encountered the enemy, we were all very anxious to be sent out as scouts, in order to have a chance of trying our hand on the foe.

It was on the 20th of June, if I remember correctly, that one of our officers, Lieutenant Toki, started out, with half a company of men under him, to reconnoitre the enemy about Lwanni-chiao, but did not come across any Russians. He left a small detachment as a rear-guard and started back. Unexpectedly two Russian scouts appeared between his men and this rear-guard. They were surrounded, but offered stubborn resistance with bayonets and would not surrender. They were fired at, and fell, though still alive. They were our first captives and we were anxious to question them. They were placed on straw mat stretchers made on the spot to suit the occasion, and carried in triumph to the side of a brook at a little distance from the headquarters of our regiment. This was our first bag of captives. The men swarmed around the poor Russians, eager to enjoy the first sight of prisoners-of-war. Presently came the aide-de-camp of the brigade and an interpreter. The two captives were put in different places and examined separately. This was according to the recognized rule of separate cross-questioning, so that the real truth may be inferred through comparison and synthesis of the different assertions of different prisoners. In examining them, the first questions put are, what army, division, etc., do they belong to, who are their high commanders, where did they stay the previous night, how is the morale of their army, etc. Even when we have no time to go through all these questions, we must find out what they belong to, in order to ascertain the disposition of the enemy's forces. If, for instance, they say they belong to the First Regiment of Infantry sharpshooters, we can infer from that statement who the commander is and what is his probable plan of campaign.

Our surgeons gave the captives proper medical care and comforted them, saying: "Depend upon

肉
弾

it, we shall take good care of you. Be at your ease and answer truthfully whatever is asked of you."

The surgeons told us that both Russians had been shot through the chest and would not live an hour longer, and therefore that it was advisable to put only a few important questions while they retained consciousness. One of the examiners said: "Of what regiment and of what place are you?"

The poor captive answered, gaspingly: "The Twenty-sixth Regiment of Infantry sharpshooters." "Who is the commander of your division?" "Don't know." The interpreter expostulated. "You can't say you don't know. You ought to know the name of your own commander."

The captive showed his sincerity in his countenance; probably he meant what he said. He was breathing with difficulty, and blood was running out of his mouth.

"Please give me a drink of water."

I was standing nearest to him and obtained a glass of spring water. When I gave him to drink he would not even look at it.

"There is boiled water in my bottle; give me that."

I did as was requested. I do not know whether this Russian, even in his last moments, disdained to receive a drink from the enemy, but I was struck with his carefulness in observing the rules of hygiene and not drinking unboiled water. Because of this strength of character, he had bravely fought with our scouting party until he was struck down. But he was not the only Russian soldier who did not know the name of his commanding general. Afterwards when I had chances of cross-questioning a large number of captives, I found out that the majority of them were equally ignorant. Moreover, they did not know for what or for whom they were fighting. Nine men out of ten would say that they had been driven to the field without knowing why or wherefore.

No more time was allowed for questioning this captive. He became whiter and whiter, breathed with more and more difficulty; his end was fast approaching. The surgeon said: "Do you suffer? Have you anything to say?"

At these kind words he raised his head a little and said, with tears: "I have left my wife and one child in my country; please let them know how I died."

He breathed his last soon afterward. This man sacrificed his life without knowing what for. To be driven to the far-away East, to be captured by the enemy, and die thinking of his wife and child! He brought tears of sympathy to our eyes. He was honorably buried under a cross, and Chaplain Toyama offered Buddhist prayers.

The other captive was different in his attitude

肉
彈

and manners, and we were far from pitying him. Of course we had no personal enmity toward him, or toward any one of the Russian fighters, and therefore we were quite ready to pity those worthy of pity, to love those worthy of love. But what do you think we found in this particular one?

When the interpreter asked the man, "Where is your regiment stationed now?" his answer was something like this: "Shut up! I don't know. The Japanese are cruel; they are merciless to those who surrender. Give me some soup to drink; give me some tobacco."

This rude remark and behavior came, not from true courage, that does not fear the enemy, but from sheer insolence. Other men whom we captured later were worthy of a similar description.

Although the Russians had been badly defeated at Nanshan, they did not yet know what was the real ability of the Japanese army; and relying upon the so-called invincible strength of Port Arthur behind them, they made light of their small-statured enemy. They were also like the frogs in the well,[1] and did not know anything of our great victory of Chinlien-chêng and that the Russians had been entirely expelled from Korea. Even when they were told of these facts, they would not believe them. Boasting of the mere size of their country and army,

[1] Japanese proverb: The frog in the well knows not the great ocean.

74

when were the Russians to awake from their deluding dreams?

Day and night we tried hard to find out the enemy's whereabouts. One time a large reconnoitring detachment was sent out, when they came across a body of Russian cavalry, many of whom were killed and their horses captured by our men. The enemy also was watching us incessantly, and away on the top of Waitu-shan a corps of observation equipped with telescopes was seen constantly giving signals with black flags. Sometimes they would send out scouts dressed as Chinese natives to spy our advance lines. At first we were deceived by their appearance and some of our patrols were killed in an unguarded moment. Then we learned to be more careful and did not allow even the real Chinese to cross our line. Upon one occasion the mayor of the village in front of us asked for permission to come within the Japanese line, on the ground that they were greatly inconvenienced by not being allowed to cross it. After that the headquarters of the brigade appointed a special committee to investigate into individual cases, and only those Chinese who had families or relatives living inside the line were allowed to come over. Of course the Chinese would do almost anything for money. There were many who had been bribed by the Russians to become spies. They caused us a great deal of damage in spite of every possible precaution.

第九

肉
弾

Thus we were kept busy with necessary preparations for an actual engagement, waiting for the right opportunity to present itself. For strategic reasons, we did not take an offensive attitude for some time, leaving everything to the choice of the enemy, with the mere precaution against a surprise by the Russians. Meanwhile the enemy's navy appeared near Hsiaoping-tao and Hehshih-chiao and tried to find out our place of encampment by firing at us at random. At last the time came for us to begin active operations. On the 26th of June, the besieging army commenced hostilities and our regiment participated in the battle of Waitu-shan and Kenzan.

第十

OUR FIRST BATTLE AT WAITU-SHAN

FOR about thirty days we had waited for a good opportunity, fortifying ourselves strongly, and engaged in constant skirmishes with the enemy. There was, however, one thing that we could not permit, and that was that the enemy was able to look down into our camp from various high points in their position. They occupied Waitu-shan, 372 metres in height, Shuangting-shan, a double-peaked mountain, of 352 metres, and a nameless mountain, which we afterward christened Kenzan, or Sword Mountain, higher and steeper than the first two. These mountains were secure from our attack, and from these eminences the enemy could spy us very well and comfortably. They set up fine telescopes on these places and took in what we were doing in our camp, in the Bay of Talien, and in Dalny. This was a great disadvantage to us. The longer they occupied those heights, the longer our necessary preparations at the rear must be delayed and the right opportunity to advance and strike might be lost. So it was an urgent necessity to take these places

77

肉
彈

of vantage, and also to take Hsiaoping-tao in order
to prevent the enemy's warships from threatening
our defenses of Talien Bay. This was the reason
for our first battle, an attack on Waitu-shan.

This was not a severe battle; its object was simply
to drive away the enemy occupying these heights.
Because of the natural strength of the place, the
Russians had not done much to protect or fortify it,
and it was comparatively easy for us to attack. But
this was the first fight for us, and we fought it with
special fervor and determination.

Late in the night of the 25th, the last day of
our defensive attitude, when the watch-fires of the
camps were going out, and the occasional braying
of donkeys added to the solitude of the hour, a
secret order was brought to us to begin at once to
prepare for fighting. Why was this message given
at midnight? Because of fear of the natives. It
had been arranged that our march and attack should
begin on the 24th, but when we began to make
preparations for starting, we soon found reason to
suspect the natives of having informed the enemy
of our movements and intentions. So we stopped
for that day, and daybreak of the 26th was assigned for the attack, so that we could begin our
march before the natives knew anything of it. That
night I could hardly sleep for excitement; I tossed
and fretted in bed, pictured to myself the battle of
the morrow, or talked nonsense with the comrade

in the nearest bed. I saw the occasional flickering of small fires in the dark and knew that not a few were awake, smoking and cogitating.

Very soon the whole atmosphere of the camp was filled with quiet activity; officers and men jumped out of bed and began to fold tents and overcoats as noiselessly as possible. Putting on our creaking knapsacks with the utmost caution, we crept with stealthy tread across the grass, and gathering at one spot stacked our rifles. The sky was inky black with summer clouds; the bayonets and the stars on our caps were the only things that glittered in the dark. Though their eyes were dull and sleepy, all were eager and determined in spirit.

"Have you left nothing behind? Are all the fires out?"

All at once the whole line became silent and began to move on at the command "March silently." We had to keep very still until we were fairly out of the village, so that when the Chinese got up in the morning they would be surprised at our absence. This was the time for us to put in practice the quiet march, in which we had had much previous training. Even a month's stay in the place had endeared to us, to some extent, the rivers and hills; the village had come to seem a sort of second home. How could we be indifferent to the tree that had given us shelter and to the stream that had given us drink? Among the villagers there was an old man by the

79

name of Chodenshin, a descendant of a refugee of the Ming dynasty. He had helped us very faithfully, drawing water in the morning, and kindling fires in the evening. This good man discovered that we were going, and worked all the night through to help us. When we began the march, he came to the end of the village to see us off. Of course we could not forget such a man, and every now and then we used to talk about his faithful services.

The morning mist enshrouded the sky and the sun had not yet risen. The Sun Flag was at the head of our long line of march. Far away toward the right flank several shots were heard. Had the battle really begun?

At this moment both the right and left columns of our army began action, the right one to attack the height to the southwest of the village of Pantu, and the left to attack the enemy's entrenchments on the heights to the east of the village of Lwanni-chiao, that is, from the 368-metre hill (Kenzan) on the north, along the ridge to Shuangting-shan in the south.

Our — that is, the middle — division of the left column was assigned to attack Waitu-shan. We marched quietly, binding the horses' tongues, furling our flag, and trailing our arms. When we came close to the place, the enemy poured a fierce volley on us from the top of the hill and offered stubborn resistance. Brave, worthy foe! We responded with

80

a brisk fire and sent showers of bullets and shells.
They were on an eminence and we at the foot of the
hill; their shots fell like rain on our heads and raised
dust at our feet. At last the curtain of our first act
was raised. This was our first chance to compare
our strength with theirs. The coming and going of
bullets and shells became fiercer and fiercer as time
went on. The exploding gas of the smokeless powder filled the whole field with a vile smell. The
sound of the opening and shutting of the breech-
blocks of the guns, the sound of empty cartridges
jumping out, the moaning of the bullets, the groaning of the shells, wounding as they fell, how stirring,
how sublime! The cry "Forward! Forward!" rises
on every side. Steep hills and sword-like rocks are
braved and climbed at a quick, eager pace; the
cartridges rattle in their cases; the sword jumps;
the heart dances. March and shoot, shoot and
march! The enemy's shot rain hard; our bullets
fly windward. The battle has become fierce.

Until we have pierced the body of the foe with our
shot, we must continue to harass them with our fire.
The bayonet is the finishing touch; the guns must
play a large part in a battle. So, therefore, we must
be very careful in shooting. When the fighting once
begins, we begin to dance from the top of the head
to the tip of the toe, we lose ourselves in excitement,
but that does not do. It is very difficult to act coolly,
but the aiming and the pulling of the trigger must

肉
彈

be done deliberately, however noisy the place may be, however bloody the scene. This is the secret determining who shall be the victor.

> "Pull the trigger as carefully and gently
> As the frost falls in the cold night,"

is the poem teaching the secret. Such a cool, deliberate shot is sure to hit the mark. The enemy fall one after another. Then follows the final assault (tokkwan), then the triumphal tune is sung, the Kimi ga yo[1] is played, and Banzai to the Emperor is shouted. This is the natural order of events.

The spirit of the men on the firing line improved steadily; the battle-field became more and more active. The number of the wounded increased moment after moment. Cries of "A-a!" sounded from every side, as the bullets found their mark and men fell to earth unconscious.

The final opportunity was fast coming toward us; the enemy began to waver. One foot forward, another foot backward, they were in a half-hearted condition. 'T is time for "Tokkan! Tokkan!" [2] the

---

[1] Kimi ga yo, the national hymn, which may be roughly translated thus: —

> May our Lord's dominion last,
> Till ten thousand years have passed
> And the stone
> On the shore at last has grown
> To a great rock, mossy and gray.

[2] The words tokkwan, translated "final assault," and this word, Tokkan, meaning the war-cry, belong close together in thought as in sound. The "Tokkan!" which has been retained

82

time for a shout like the beating on a broken bell and for a dash at the foe. Lo! a fierce rain of rifle-shot falls, followed by the shouting of a hundred thunders; mountains and valleys shake; heaven and earth quake. Captain Murakami, commander of the company, shouting tremendously and brandishing his long sword, rushes forward. All the soldiers follow his example and pierce the enemy's line, shouting, screaming, dancing, and jumping. This done, the Russians turn their backs on us and run for their lives, leaving behind arms, powder, caps, etc. How cleverly and quickly they scamper away! That at least deserves our praise.

Waitu-shan became ours once for all. We did not fight a very hard fight, but this our first success was like a stirrup cup. "Medetashi![1] medetashi!" We raised our hearty Banzai to the morning sky at eight o'clock on the 26th of June.

in the translation, is onomatopoetic, and gives force to the words that immediately follow it.

[1] "Medetashi!" Glorious!

THE OCCUPATION OF KENZAN

WAITU–SHAN being taken with ease, the emboldened thousands of our soldiers now began to chase the fleeing enemy along the long, narrow path leading from Ling-shui-ho-tzu to the 368-metre hill, that is, Kenzan. The object of this march was to attack the Russians occupying Kenzan, and our men were more eager and enthusiastic than ever, and fully expected to take this hill with one single stroke.

Kenzan is a very steep, rocky, rugged peak, and the path on our side was particularly steep and rugged, so much so that one man on the path could prevent thousands of men from either climbing or descending. This hill had had no name originally, but the Russians themselves christened it Quin Hill. After the place was taken, General Nogi gave it the name of Kenzan, "Sword Hill," after the famous steep hill Tsurugi[1]-ga-miné of Shikoku, near our home barracks, in order to perpetuate the fame of the regiment that took this steep place. We did not know at first how large a Russian force was sta-

[1] *Tsurugi*, sword.

tioned there. We had only ascertained that there were some infantry and more than ten guns for its defense.

第十一

Our regiment, as the reserve force, went round the foot of Waitozan and stopped in the cultivated fields near the seashore. At this time it was burning hot in Liaotung; moreover, there was no stream of water to moisten our mouths, no trees or bushes beyond the village to give us shade. Our position was even without grass, and we were exposed to the red-hot-poker-like rays of the sun, which seemed to pierce through our caps and melt our heads. We, however, consoled ourselves with the idea that this horrible fire-torture would not last long, and that soon we should have a chance of real fighting. But we remained in the same position from 9 A.M. till 3 P.M., all the hottest hours of the day. Far away to the left was visible the rippling water of the eastern sea — how we longed for a cold bath before going forward to die on the battle-field! We could not help our mouths watering at the distant sight of the sea!

After a while, a Russian gunboat appeared near Hsiaoping-tao, an island to our left, and began to fire at our reserve force. Many circles of smoke were scattered high in the air, the air itself made a whirling sound, and the shot fell on our position with a tremendous noise. Shot after shot, sound after sound! Some would hit rocks, emit sparks, spread smoke around, and the rock itself would fly in pieces.

85

肉
弾

Seen from a safe distance, it is a heart-stirring sight, but we would not have welcomed a real hit. Nearly all this shot came very near us, but fortunately none of us was wounded. Soon we began to hear the booming of guns and cannon in the direction of Kenzan; and we knew the attack had begun. We were anxiously longing to march and join the battle.

How eagerly we welcomed the order, "Forward, march!" As soon as it was heard, all the men jumped up with a spring and turned their eyes to the colonel's face. The commander's brave bearing is always looked up to by his men as their pattern. Especially in a critical moment, when the issue of the day is to be settled, his undaunted attitude and steady gaze will alone inspire his men with the courage and energy which lead them to victory.

Now we were to march. Our heavy knapsacks would have hindered our activity. The men hurried to put about a day's ration into a long sack to be fastened to the back, and fixed their overcoats to their shoulders. I pulled out two or three cigarettes from a package and started at once. Without any special order from anybody, our pace became faster and faster — we marched along a long road toward the place where the roar of cannon and rifles was rising. We came nearer and nearer to the noise of the battle-line. When we reached the actual spot, how our hearts leaped!

The steep hill occupied by the enemy rose in front

86

of us almost perpendicularly. Our first line was incessantly exchanging fire with the Russians. As the
fighting became harder and harder, the number of
the wounded increased in proportion; they were
carried to the rear in quick succession. Bloodstained men on stretchers, wounded soldiers walking with difficulty, supporting themselves on rifles
— the sight of these unfortunate ones made us
fresh men the more eager to avenge them.

The struggle became still fiercer. Our artillery
tried hard to silence the enemy's guns; our infantry were clambering up the steep height one after
the other — they would stop and shoot, then climb
a little and stop again. The whole sky was covered
with gray clouds — white and black smoke rose in
volumes; shells fell on the ground like a hail-storm.
After a short time, our superior artillery effectively
silenced three or four of the enemy's guns. Our infantry came quite close to the enemy, when two mines
exploded before them. Our men were enveloped in
black smoke and clouds of dust — we feared great
damage was done. Strange to tell, however, not one
of our men had fallen when the smoke-cloud cleared
away. The enemy had wasted a large quantity of precious powder with the mere result of raising a dust!

The Russians tried to hinder our pressing on, not
only by these exploding mines, but also by repeated
volleys from the mountain-top. This latter scheme
was carried out so incessantly that we could hardly

肉
彈
turn our faces toward the enemy or raise our heads comfortably. On and on, however, we marched without fear or hesitancy. A small company of men at the head of the line would clamber up the rocks and precipices, ready for annihilation; encouraged by their example, larger forces would break in upon the enemy like a flood. Stepping on mine-openings and braving rifle and cannon fire coming from front and side, the extreme danger and difficulty of their attack was beyond description. The enemy resisted desperately; this Heaven-protected steep Kenzan was too important for them to give up.

Suddenly a tremendous shout arose throughout our whole line; all the officers, with drawn swords and bloodshot eyes, rushed into the enemy's forts, shouting and yelling and encouraging their men to follow. A hell-like struggle ensued, in which bayonet clashed against bayonet, fierce shooting was answered by fierce shooting, shouts and yells were mingled with the groans of the wounded and dying. The battle soon became ours, for, in spite of their desperate resistance, the enemy took to their heels, leaving behind them many mementos of their defeat. Banzai was shouted two or three times; joy and congratulation resounded on the heights of Kenzan, which was now virtually ours. The Flag of the Rising Sun was hoisted high at the top of the hill. This stronghold once in our hands, shall we ever give it back to the enemy?

第
十
二

COUNTER–ATTACKS ON KENZAN

KENZAN once in our hands, Shuangting-shan and its vicinity soon became ours. Through the smoke our colors were seen flying over the forces now occupying these places, whose thunder-like triumphal shouts echoed above the winds. This Shuangting-shan was as important as Kenzan — neither position must remain in the hands of the enemy. But Shuangting-shan was not strongly fortified and the Russians could not hold it long against us. It was an easy prey for us. "When one wild goose is frightened, the whole line of wild geese goes into disorder; when one company wavers, the whole army is defeated," so says the old expression. When the Russians lost Kenzan, which they had relied upon so much, Shuangting-shan fell like a dead leaf, and Hsiaoping-tao also became ours. This island is to the left of the foot of Shuang-ting-shan and, as I have already told you, Russian ships had appeared in that neighborhood and attacked us on the flank; this attempt at piercing our side with a sharp spear was very effective. These ships were driven back into Port Arthur more than once by our fleet; but as soon as they found a chance, they would come back and bombard our flank. During the battle of the 26th, three or four gunboats of the enemy were in that vicinity; they greatly hindered our attacks on Kenzan and Shuangting-shan. So the left wing of our left column was ordered to take the island, and it soon fell into our hands. Thus the whole of the first line of the enemy's defense about Port Arthur came entirely under our flag.

Every detachment of our army was successful in its attack of the 26th, and this gave us an enormous advantage for the future development of our plan of campaign. We were now in a position to look down upon the enemy's movements, from those same heights whence they once had espied our doings. It is, therefore, no wonder that the Russians tried to recover this vantage ground. It is said that General Stoessel ordered his whole army to recover, at whatever cost, this Kenzan, which, he said, was indispensable for the defense of Port Arthur. This was quite natural for them. But we Japanese had determined not to give up the place to the enemy, whatever counter-attack, whatever stratagem, might be brought to bear. If they were ready for a great sacrifice, we were equally willing to accept the sacrifice. Brave Russians, come and attack us twice or thrice, if you are anxious to have regrets afterward! What they did was "to keep the tiger off the front gate and not to know that the wolf was already at the back door."

The long, summer-day's sun was going down, a dismal gray light enveloped heaven and earth; after the battle warm, unpleasant winds were sweeping over bloodstained grass, and the din of war of a short time before was followed by an awful silence, except for the scattered reports of rifles, with thin, dull, spiritless sound. This was the repulsed enemy's random shooting to give vent to their anger and regret — it was quite an amusement for us. All of a sudden, dark clouds were vomited by mountain peaks, the whole sky became black in a moment, lightning and thunder were followed by bullet-like drops of rain; nature seemed to repeat the same desperate, bloody scene that we had presented a short while before. This battle of the elements was an additional hardship for our men, — they had not even trees for shelter, — all looked like rats drenched in water! We spent the night on this mountain in the rain, listening to the neighing of our horses at its foot.

A severe battle is usually followed by a heavy storm or shower. When the battle is at its height, the sky is darkened with powder-smoke and the whole scene is dismal and dreary. Presently a heavy shower and deafening thunders come to wash away all impurities of the battle-field. This rain is called "the tears of joy for the victor, and the tears of sor-

y

第十二

y

91

肉
弾

row for the defeated;" it is also the tears of mourning for the dead comrades. Such a stormy night was
almost sure to be utilized by the enemy to recover
the lost position. But we were not off our guard
after our victory, as the enemy may have imagined
— the roar of thunder or the fall of rain did not
make us less vigilant. Each time they visited us,
we were sure to dismiss them at the gate, thanking
them for their fruitless visit. Once we occupy a
place, a line of strict vigilance is spread all around,
ready to meet the enemy's counter-surprise at any
moment. This is what we call "tightening the
string of the helmet in victory." [1]

Seven days had elapsed after our taking Kenzan
and Shuangting-shan, when the enemy began a
counter-attack, at mid-day of the 3d of July. They
seemed to be trying to recover Kenzan with an overwhelming force. About eight or nine hundred of
their infantry pressed straight on from Wangchia-
tun; their artillery took up their position in and
about Tashik-tung and began to fire at us with
great energy. We had been expecting this all the
time and were not surprised. All our guns and rifles
were concentrated on their front; they were brave
enough to rush on in spite of this shower of shot.
But our fire was too much for them; they "fell
like a row of ninepins." The officer at their head

[1] A saying of Iyeyasu, the great soldier and lawgiver, — "in
the moment of victory, tighten your helmet-strings."

flourished his long sword high in the air and furiously rushed toward us; but he too fell. At each volley they fell like autumn leaves in the wind. The remnant of the enemy thought it impossible to face us; they ran back into the valleys in complete disorder. Their infantry had thus retreated, but the battery was not silenced so easily. For some time longer it held on and fired at our centre vigorously. Perhaps the sight of the retreating infantry made the artillerymen lose courage; the noise of their firing became less and less; soon the whole line of battle became as quiet as a dream. We shouted Banzai again and again. The enemy's first effort to regain Kenzan had failed!

The Russians were so persistent in their attempt at recovering the lost position, that, soon after this severe defeat, about the same number of infantry as before made their appearance on Taiko-shan. Their band playing vigorously, they approached our first line. When the distance between the two parties became only seven or eight hundred metres, they deployed, shouted "Woola!" very loud, and rushed on us bravely, encouraged by the sound of fife and drum. We met them with a violent, rapid fire, killing both those who advanced and those who retreated. One of our detachments also took the offensive. This again was too much for the enemy; they took to their heels and went back toward Taiko-shan. In spite of the clear fact that it was impossible for them to defeat us, they repeated one attack after another, making a fresh sacrifice of men each time, fully determined to recover Kenzan. This tenacity of purpose was truly worthy of a great Power and deserves our admiration. Just as we have our loyal and brave "Yamato-damashii," they have their own undaunted courage peculiar to the Slav race. "The tiger's roar causes storms to rise and the dragon's breath gathers clouds in the sky." Each of the contending parties had a worthy foe with which to compare its strength.

At one o'clock on the morning of the following day (the 4th), the enemy broke through the darkness of midnight and surprised us on Kenzan with a forlorn-hope detachment. This movement was so quick and so clever! not a blade of grass, not a stone was disturbed — they clambered up the steep ascent without a noise, and quite suddenly they killed our sentries and rushed into our camp in a dense crowd, with loud shouts, flourishing their swords and brandishing their rifles. A scene of great confusion and desperate struggle ensued; it was pitch dark and we could not tell friend from foe — the only thing we could do was to cut and thrust as much as possible without knowing at whom. We could not see anything, but each could hear and feel the heavy fall to the ground of his own antagonist. Once again our defense was too strong even for this assaulting party, who went down the hill in disappointment, though without confusion. We were all astonished at their valor and perseverance. Even those who were left behind wounded would try and resist us with rifle or sword. One of them, in particular, who was seriously wounded and on the brink of death, raised his drooping head and smiled a ghastly smile of defiance and determination.

Such a clever, well-planned surprise having failed, we thought that probably they had given up any idea of further attack on us. Contrary to our expectation, however, they still clung to the object of recovering Kenzan by some means. At the dawn of the same morning, they tried an open attack with a large force. This assault was particularly fierce. This time they showed even more determination than before; their artillery kept up a continuous fire, while the infantry made their advance under its cover. The number of men on their first line was constantly increased, and they seemed determined to wrest Kenzan from us at any cost. In spite of our advantageous position, in spite of our experience in repeated repulse of the enemy, the assault of this large body of Russians was far from easy for us to break. But we too had increased our numbers and had improved our defenses as much as possible, in expectation of just such an attack. Consequently this was almost as severe a fight as our attack on Kenzan.

The artillery of the enemy increased in strength hour after hour and occupied the heights connecting

第十二

肉
弾
Wangchia-tun, Mautao-kou, Antsu-ling, and so on; their main strength was directed to Kenzan, and also to our infantry position in general. Their way of pouring shrapnel on us was most energetic, and they proved themselves better marksmen than ever. Without the intermission of even a minute or a second, their shot and shells rained on us in a heavy shower. From early morning both our artillery and infantry kept up a rapid fire and tried hard to prevent the enemy from coming nearer, fully determined not to allow them to enter, even one step, into the place we had once taken with our blood. In particular, those who were stationed at Kenzan had the hardest of times; they stood firm under the enemy's fierce fire and checked with great difficulty an attempt to rush their position. Sometimes they were hard pressed and in danger of giving way; at such times the officers in front would stir them up and cry, "Shoot! Shoot!" staring at the enemy with angry eyes and spitting foam from their mouths! The men kept their eyes fixed steadily on the enemy, their hands at work incessantly with magazine and trigger. They strained all their energy and power and did not economize powder, of which they are so careful at other times.

The firing from both sides became more and more violent and quick, so that birds could not have found space to fly, or animals places for hiding. Thousands and thousands of shot and shell crossed in the

96

air and made a dull sound in the heavy-laden atmosphere; the whole heaven and earth seemed the scene of the frantic rage of demons, and we could not prophesy when this scene would come to an end. The enemy's artillery fire was very strong; their *time* shells would fly to us in bundles, explode over our heads, and kill and wound our men mercilessly. The explosion of their spherical shells would hurl up earth and sand before and behind our skirmish line, raising a thick black and white smoke at the spot. The struggle of our artillery to resist such a violent, incessant attack was beyond description. They were sometimes obliged to change their position for a while. The issue of the day was still hanging in the balance; the enemy's forces were reinforced from time to time by fresh men—they renewed the attack again and again. On our side, too, a part of our general reserve was placed on the line of battle; moreover, several companies of heavy artillery were sent out from Pantao to Hwangni-chuan, Tashang-tun, and their vicinity. Also, the marine heavy artillery corps was stationed at Shakako in the south. With this increase of strength on both sides, each party threatened to annihilate the other. The fight of the day became more and more desperate; the boom of cannon and rifle lasted from dawn till dusk — still it did not lessen in its volume. The enemy seemed anxious to take advantage of the good effect of their fire to make an assault on us

第十二

under its cover. The sharper their attack, the more watchful we became, and each time we dealt a correspondingly severe counter-attack.

The melancholy rays of the setting sun shone upon the dismal scene of the battle-field, with a background of dark gray which added to the sadness of the sight. This sadness, of course, was associated with our anxiety about the issue of the struggle. Was the battle of this day to cease without any result? Nay, the enemy would not give up the attack with the arrival of night; on the contrary, because they had a plan for a great night assault on us, they continued their firing from morning till evening, in order to exhaust us both in body and resources. We were sure that this was their plan, and so at night we waited for their coming with more vigilance and watchfulness. As was expected, the enemy's whole line began to move late at night and attempted to storm Kenzan and recover the place with one tremendous stroke. They came upon us in rage and fury: their bayonets glittered in the dark like the reflection of the sun on ice and frost; their "Woola" sounded like the roar of hundreds of wild beasts. "Now is the time for us to show them what we're made of!" With this idea in all our minds, we began with one accord to shower on them an accurate fire; nearly all the shot told. We were almost certain that the enemy would be defeated before so sure a fire. Their cry of "Woola" became less and less loud; the flowers of their swords also faded away in the dark. At last the whole place became perfectly quiet, so that we could hear the melancholy note of summer insects singing in the grass, and the groaning of the wounded Russians left on the field. Up in the sky, thick clouds hung heavy and low, threatening to begin to rain at any moment. Our eyes rained first a drop or two in spite of ourselves — for our comrades who had died in this battle.

Later, when all the information was gathered, we found that the number of the Russians that began the attack early in the morning was about one thousand; it was gradually reinforced and became five thousand, and at last it was more than ten thousand. Added to this, some gun-boats of the enemy appeared off the coast of Lungwang-tang and fired vehemently on our centre and left wing. Even this large, combined force of the army and navy could not accomplish their cherished object — all their stratagems and tricks were of no avail against us. After this fourth and hardest assault, they seemed to lose courage and hope; no further attack was made on Kenzan; the only thing they continued to do was to reconnoitre our camp, and to direct slow firing on us both day and night, accompanied by an occasional night assault on a small scale, which seemed intended to cover and protect the defensive works which they were putting up in great hurry along the heights of Taipo-shan.

第十三

ON THE DEFENSIVE

WHAT an irksome, tantalizing business is defense! We may be quite ready to march and fight, both in morale and in material preparations, and yet we must wait until the right opportunity arrives. The sword hanging from the belt may moan from idleness, the muscles of the arm sigh from inactivity, and yet we have to wait till the proper time comes. But defense is the first step toward offense. We must first try every possible means, on this line of vigilant defense, to ascertain minutely and accurately the condition of the enemy, and to find out the arrangement of their men, before we lay our plans and begin a march and attack. So, therefore, our defense is like the dragon concealing itself in a pond for a while, and our march its gathering clouds and fogs around itself and ascending to heaven. So, then, I propose here to tell you a little about the actual condition of our line of defense after the battle of Kenzan.

A strong army of fourteen battalions and twenty-four guns had tried a hard and desperate assault on our position, to recover Kenzan "at whatever cost," to use General Stoessel's expression. But their scheme of reprisals was of no use. They retreated far back toward Shwangtai-kou and Antsu-ling on the north, and Taipo-shan and Laotso-shan on the south, and there along the heights they put up strong works of defense, planning to make a firmer stand there than at Kenzan. And we remained in exactly the same position as before, not even an inch of ground was given back to the enemy; our line stretched from Antsu-ling in the north, with Lwanni-chiao, Kenzan, Hwangni-chuan, and Tashang-tun in the middle, to Shuangting-shan in the south. Our regiment was to watch over the heights to the north-east of Hwangni-chuan and Tashang-tun, and on the very first day we began to dig with picks and shovels. As compared with our experience in Chang-chia-tun, we were much nearer the enemy, and, moreover, we had to make our works much stronger, knowing that the enemy would be sure to try an occasional assault on us, notwithstanding their re-peated defeats in the attempt to recover Kenzan. We had no time to give our men rest after their hard, continuous fighting. We could not leave our gate-way wide open for thieves and burglars, however anxious we were to rest our men. The urgent neces-sity of the case did not allow sympathetic consid-eration for their exhaustion. The brave soldiers themselves did not think of any repose; day and

肉
弾

night they carried the sand-bags, and wire-entanglement left at Changchia-tun, along the rocky steep
path, or with no path at all, catching hold of grass-
roots or points of rock. They devoted every available
minute to putting up strong works as quickly as
possible.

Our position was on a steep, rocky, skeleton-like
mountain, over valleys with sides almost perpendicular. There were no trees to shield us from the
sun, no streams of water to moisten our parched lips.
Our only comfort was that we could see through the
mist the forts on far-away Lautieh-shan and ramparts on nearer hills and peaks, and imagine that
soon the curtain would be raised and a great living
drama again be presented on the stage. We pictured
to ourselves the joy of another valiant struggle and
wished that we might be allowed to sacrifice ourselves so completely that not a piece of our flesh be
left behind. Days passed in hard work and vain
imaginings. When the curtain of night covered the
scene, a body of black forms would climb the hill.
What were they? They were fresh men to take the
places of those exhausted by the day's hard work.
Had they to work even at night? Yes, on the line
of defense this night work was the more important.
In the daytime the enemy's artillery would fire
and try to find out where we were working, and
therefore steady progress was impossible. To make
up the time lost we had to work at night. Looking

at the distant smoke rising from the camp-fires of the enemy, our men dug earth, piled up stones, carried sand, filled sacks, and planted stakes for wire-entanglements. In doing this we had to try to make as little noise as possible, and of course could not smoke. Even the lighting of a cigarette might give occasion for the enemy to fire at us. At two or three o'clock in the morning, we were still working hard, in spite of heavy rain or furious storm. The men did all this without complaining, ungrudgingly; they only thought of doing their very best for their country, and for their sovereign. They truly deserve the heartfelt thanks and praises of the nation.

In the small hours of the morning the body of pioneers would rest their arms awhile. Even then there were some who stood straight like statues with their guns on their shoulders, straining their eyes toward the enemy. The duty of the sentinels was also far from easy. Exposed to the night wind of the peninsula they would smile and say: "It's very cool to-night! Shall we have another night assault as usual?"

We did not know certainly where the enemy's artillery was stationed, but they would fire into the valley where the staff officers had pitched their tents, as if in search of us. It was on the 15th of July, if I remember correctly, that a big ball came flying, exploded with a tremendous noise, shattered rocks, threw up stones, raised dark yellow smoke, and shook the earth. We had been accustomed only to field-gun balls: this was our first experience of such a huge one. We were greatly astonished. Probably the enemy had hauled a navy gun up to Lungwang-tang and fired at us with that. They still seemed anxious to find a chance of recovering Kenzan, and sent us long-distance balls diligently. All our battalions, therefore, agreed to take careful statistics, and report how many balls were sent and to what part of our line, between what and what hours. The enemy tried in vain to frighten us by shattering the rocks of Kenzan with long-distance shot. Seen from a distance, the explosion of shrapnel looks like fireworks, but to be under such a shower of fire is not particularly pleasant.

There was one thing that puzzled us very much. Every day, almost at the same hour, they would fire at us with special zeal; their aim was always directed to our headquarters and sometimes they would inflict upon us unexpected damage. We thought, of course, there must be some secret in this mysterious act of the enemy's, but it was not at all easy to find out that secret. After a long and careful investigation, the following wonderful and detestable fact came to light.

The Chinese natives were in the habit of driving cows or sheep up to the hills at the back of our line of vigilance and giving signals to the Russians from this great distance. Their code was to indicate the direction or village to be fired at by a black cow, a flock of sheep, etc. Our experience at Changchia-tun had fully warned us of the dangerous quality of the Chinese, who would give up even their lives for money. But this time they did not even attempt to pass through our line, but simply drove their animals slowly up the mountain path. How could we dream that such an innocent-looking act was betraying us to the enemy! They are ignorant and greedy survivors of a fallen dynasty; they know only the value of gold and silver and do not think of national or international interests. It has never occurred to them to try to think why it was that Japan and Russia were fighting on their own farms; they were only anxious to make good the damage done to their farms and crops. Of course we had to punish these offenders very severely, though they deserved our pity, rather than our hatred. Money is the only god they worship.

It was somewhere about the 20th of this same month that some of our scouting officers went deep through the picket line of the enemy and gave a great surprise to some of their non-commissioned officers. The Japanese accomplished their object with success, and on their way back they came across three or four of the enemy's scouts. They chased the Russians about and tried to capture them, but the Russians fired at the Japanese officers in a desperate effort to make good their escape. Only one of them was left behind and captured, and our officers came back in triumph with their captive. As usual, we cross-examined the Russian, who was an infantry corporal. He bowed frequently and begged that his life might be spared, promising to tell us everything he knew. What a wretch! We wished we could give him one small dose of Japanese patriotism, which considers "duty heavier than a mountain and death lighter than a feather." [1] We hear that a Japanese soldier, who had the misfortune of being captured by the Russians at Port Arthur, rebuked and reviled, with his face flushed with anger, the Russian general before whom he was driven. On the contrary, this Russian told us every military secret he knew, in order to keep his body and soul together. When he was led on to the line of observation and told to tell us the arrangement of the Russian soldiers, he pointed out and explained it with no scruple whatever, saying to the right there was the Twenty-sixth Regiment of Infantry sharpshooters, the Twenty-eighth Regiment of the same in the middle, and what regiment on the left hand, and so on. The correspondence between his answers and the reports from scouts testified to the correctness of each. He told us all the truth he knew and we were greatly helped by him. But all the same

[1] From the Imperial Rescript to the Army and Navy. See Appendix B.

we despise him as a coward unworthy of a true soldier's society.

Let me take this opportunity of telling you about our examination of a Russian soldier captured the night after our attack on Kenzan, under a huge rock, where he was hiding himself. Our dialogue was something like this:—

"What did you expect from our attack?"

"We were afraid, and thought that the Japanese attack would be very fierce."

"Do your commanders take good care of you?"

"When we first arrived in Port Arthur they were kind and considerate to us, but recently they have not been so. For the last three months or so we have received only one third of our pay. Our rations also have been reduced one half; all the rest goes into their private pockets."

"Have those who were defeated at Nanshan gone back to Port Arthur?"

"They were not allowed to enter the great fortress; they were ordered to work on the entrenchments and live off the country, on the ground that there was no spare food to give them."

"Do you know that many of your countrymen have been sent to Japan as captives?"

"Yes, I know. Just the other day a friend of mine went to Japan as a captive."

How could the officers and commanders secure respect and obedience and faithful service from subordinates whom they did not love and take care of? Other kinds of service may be secured in other ways, but the faithful discharge of military duties, in the moment of life and death on the battle-field, can only come through the officers' loving their men as their own children, and the men's respecting their officers as their own parents. When one party is pocketing the salary and reducing the rations of the other, mercilessly involving them in unnecessary privation and hardship, how can they be respected, and how can men be expected to die for such unkind officers? The fact that the Russian soldiers pillaged the innocent natives everywhere, looting their valuables, stealing their food, and insulting their wives and daughters, finds a partial explanation in the above statement of the Russian captive.

Day after day our works on the line of defense increased in strength. All the while the Russians continued their tiresome shell assaults under cover of night, and each time they were repulsed by our men. Cannon-balls rent the air without intermission; but they were so badly aimed that we were anxious lest they might exhaust their ammunition in fruitless efforts. But aimless bullets occasionally killed or wounded our men. It is no cause of regret to die in a glorious battle, but to be wounded and killed while engaged in duties of defense, and lose the desired opportunity of joining the great fight soon to take place, was something that we did not relish. "I shall never go to the rear." "I will not be sent to the bandage-place!" These words from the lips of wounded soldiers well expressed their disappointment and regret. We can fully sympathize with their feelings.

第十四

LIFE IN CAMP

WE had relied upon our tents as a sufficient protection at least from rain and dew, but they were now in a miserable condition, torn by wind and spoiled by rain. For the sixty days since our landing we had lived in tents. All the circumstances had been against our securing other quarters. Chinese villages have seldom many houses, only three or four together, here and there; they are not at all adapted for accommodating a large army. If sometimes we happened to spend a night under the eaves of a house, sheltered from inclement weather, but smelling all the time the unsavory odor of pigs and garlic, it seemed as great a luxury as sleeping under silk comfortables in an elegant room at home. Tents were our ordinary dwelling; one sheet of canvas was everything to us, shutting off wind and rain, and making our condition far better than if we had been obliged to lie in the damp open fields with the earth as our bed. But this all-important canvas could no longer do anything except serve the purpose of covering us from the sun's rays. It allowed the merciless rain to tease us, and the angry winds to chastise us freely, for what offense we did not know. Though it kept off the scorching sun, it yielded before wind and rain. Our bodies could bear the rage of the elements; but how could we protect our rations and our guns against the weather? These things were as important to us as life itself. We had no other place of shelter, not even a tree to protect us. Crying and lamenting were of no use. If it could not be helped, we could at least sleep a good sleep exposed to rain, and lose our fatigue from the day's work in pleasant dreams. If any one could have stolen a glance at our sleeping faces on such a night, what a sight would have greeted his eyes! There we lay fully clothed, with long disheveled hair and unshaven faces, looking like beggars or mountain bandits, our tanned skins covered with dust and grime. We were terribly emaciated, our only delight was in eating. Whenever we had time, our thoughts turned to the question: What can we get to eat?

"Have you anything good?"

"No, *you* must have something nice; do give me some."

These were the usual forms of greeting when we met. Sometimes when our mouths were too lonely we roasted peas, beans, or corn and would chew them, making sounds like rats biting something hard. Such an experience showed us what a life of luxury we had been living at home.

第十四

肉弾 The capture of Dalny gave our army improved facilities for the conveyance of supplies, and we could live on without much privation, except when we were actually engaged in fighting. The soldiers received their regular rations, which they cooked for themselves. In the shadow of a rock, or at the corner of a stone wall, they might be seen cooking their food with millet stalks as fuel, waiting impatiently in the smouldering smoke for the rice to be ready. They were like happy children. The relishes were chiefly cucumber, dried radish, edible fern, dried sweet potato, or canned things. These were prized as great delicacies, as we were frequently obliged to swallow hard biscuit without water, or to welcome as a great treat half-cooked rice and one or two salt pickled plums.

Our present station was pleasanter than Chang-chia-tun. Here we had some green grass, and some lovable blossoms also smiled on us. We would pick these flowers and arrange them in empty shells or put them in our buttonholes and enjoy their fragrance. The tiny blue forget-me-nots made us sometimes fly in imagination to our dear ones at home.

We Japanese fighters had another foe besides the Russians, and it was the formidable fiend called climate. However brave a man may be, he may fall sick at any moment and have to leave the line of battle; this is being wounded by the enemy called climate, or sometimes by another called food. Exposure to the wind and rain sometimes brings about epidemics. It is hard enough to wait in wet clothes until the welcome sun comes out and dries us, but it adds greatly to the hardship to be in constant dread lest a terrible foe come and assault us at any moment. In this neighborhood there were no trees worth the name, but there was grass enough for us to thatch improvised roofs for temporary quarters. These grass roofs were sufficient to keep off the sun, but were of no use against rain and storm. In wet weather they were even worse than torn tents. We could well stand the storm of the enemy's fire, but the storm of the elements was too much for us. Our soldiers got drenched to the skin and chilled through and through; added to this their excessive work both night and day, the insufficiency of their sleep, and the drinking of the worst possible water, all combined to bring about an epidemic of dysentery, which proved a heavy drain on our forces. Attacked by this disease, I, who had been fat and strong, began to lose flesh and energy very fast and feared that I might be vanquished eventually. I was sad and grieved. Any sickness is far from welcome, but it is doubly hard to fall ill where proper medical and hygienic supplies cannot be secured. Moreover, we were expecting every day to be ordered forward to fight. Should this order come before we recovered, we must be left behind, and not partake in the glory of another

第十四

battle. This thought made us sick men still more impatient and sad. I shall never forget the kindness of three men who were my benefactors at this time. They are the two surgeons, Masaichi Yasui and Hayime Ando, and my servant, Bunkichi Takao.

In spite of the infectious nature of my trouble, these surgeons were with me all the time, and attended to my medicine, food, and nursing very carefully. They also told me interesting and amusing stories to cheer me up and to comfort me. Thanks to their efforts, I became better and was allowed to join the glorious fight and fulfill my allotted duties. Fighting together makes all men like brothers, or like fathers and sons. But this experience attached me particularly to these men, and all the time we were stationed in this place I rejoiced to labor and suffer with them. Dispersion is the ordinary rule in the battle-field; moreover, we did not know when we might be separated eternally by death. In the fierce siege of a strong fortress, death and injury cannot be limited to the men in the front lines; they may visit surgeons and other non-combatants in the rear. Not only that, but surgeons have often to risk themselves and go forward to the firing line to pick up the wounded. We never know who will be the first to die.

"If you are killed and I remain whole, I will gather all your things and keep them as a dear memento of our camp life together. If I die and you are spared, please keep a piece of my bloodstained cloak and hand it down to your posterity. My crimson blood will thus be a memento of my sincere [1] friendship to you, a symbol of my insignificant service loyally tendered to our Great Sire." Thus we talked and promised and became the best of friends. However, in the confusion of a battle-field a man does not commonly know where his particular friend fell, nor can he usually find his body. A chance meeting, whether dead or in life, was of course an exception which we could not count upon. So when the first general assault on Port Arthur was announced, I shook the hands of these two surgeons in a last farewell, never expecting to see them again in this world. Later, surrounded by the enemy, my limbs were shattered at Wangtai. A brave soldier rescued me and carried me away. I was thus removed in a strange way from the mouth of the tiger. I lost consciousness. When I recovered my senses, it was my friends Yasui and Ando who held my shattered hands and said, "We thank you." It was they who had been taking care of me.

Bunkichi Takao, my servant, was one of the company whom I had trained in the garrison. I admired his faithfulness, sincerity, and zeal. When I was transferred to the headquarters of the regiment, I made a special request to his captain and secured

第
十
四

---

[1] The word translated here "sincere" is in its primary meaning "red," hence the symbolism of the bloodstained garment.

him as my servant. Even in time of peace the relation between an officer and his servant is very close, but when once in the battle-field together their relations become still closer. It is no more master and servant, but elder and younger brother. In everything I depended upon Takao, and he in return became devotedly attached to me. He cooked for me, and brought me my food; somewhere he obtained a big water jar, carried water from a distance to fill it, and gave me the luxury of a good hot bath. In his letters to my family, we find such passages as the following: —

"Since coming to the front, we two have been quite well. Please put your heart at ease, as I am taking good care of my lieutenant. In the battle-field we don't know when we may be separated, but I shall guard my lieutenant even after death. I shall never forget his kindness. Forever and ever, please consider me as one of your family."

What sincerity and faithfulness! While I was ill he would sit up all night, forgetting his own tired-out self, to stroke my chest and rub my arms. When I asked for food in great hunger, he would chide me and soothe me as one would a baby, saying: "You cannot have anything now. When you get better, I will give you anything you want."

He paid minute attention to every detail and left nothing to be desired in nursing me. I appreciated his devotion and was very grateful to him. Later, when I was wounded, Takao was no longer my servant. He also was wounded, but heard of my injury as he was being sent to the rear. He tried hard to search me out in this field hospital or that, but he could not find me and was greatly grieved, as I have since learned. Heaven seemed willing to spare the life of such a sincere man as Takao. He had the good fortune to come home in the final triumph. He was wounded twice, ordered to the front thrice, and is now well known as a loyal servant and a veteran warrior. Frequently he discharged with success the important duties of orderly, his undaunted courage and quick sagacity always helping him in moments of difficulty.

Although our camp was, as you have seen, exposed to merciless attacks of storm, heat, and sickness, and the enemy's projectiles were frequent visitors to beguile our lonely moments, nevertheless the morale of men and officers improved day by day. They were hungering and thirsting for an early chance to assume the offensive.

第十四

SOME BRAVE MEN AND THEIR MEMORIAL

THE poor Russians who were hopelessly invested in Port Arthur were being driven back into a smaller and smaller space every day, so that of necessity they tried desperately to break through our line and enlarge their sphere of activity. Their repeated repulse at Kenzan had apparently discouraged further attempts at retaking the hill, but almost every day they attacked some spot on our line with more or less spirit. However, they were never once successful, and their efforts resulted only in the loss of ammunition and men.

About the 10th of July, we sent some advance patrols to a steep hill in front of our line, which we named Iwayama, Rocky Hill. On this spot the enemy's scouts had made their appearance frequently and tried to spy out the condition of our defenses. So we drove them away, and put up our own line of outposts there. It was on the 16th of July, while it was yet pitch dark, that Lieutenant Sugimura and a handful of men were ordered to this spot. Even in summer the night breeze on the continent is cool, and the chilly wind swept their faces through the darkness and rustled the grass. The men, reduced to skin and bone, and with morbidly sensitive nerves from their continued insufficiency of sleep, lay watching through the darkness with straining eyes, occasionally putting an ear to the ground to listen for footsteps, thinking that the enemy must be sure to come on such a night. Suddenly the sentinel's cry "The enemy!" was followed by the lieutenant's order "Deploy skirmishers!" Cool and courageous, Sugimura faced the attack with an eager determination to defend this important spot to the very last. The enemy encircled them from three sides, and they were many more than the Japanese, though the exact number could not be ascertained in the dark. Moreover, the enemy brought machine-guns and attacked the Japanese fiercely on the flank. These dreadful engines of destruction the Russians relied upon as their best means of defense. Our army had faced them at Nanshan and been mowed down by hundreds and thousands. Imagine Lieutenant Sugimura, with only a handful of soldiers, fearlessly brandishing his long sword and directing his men to fight this formidable enemy. The fate of the small group of defenders, surrounded by the enemy on three sides, was entirely in Sugimura's hand. He was so brave and his men so valiant that they fought on for two hours and did not yield even

第十五

肉
弾

an inch of ground. In spite of their overwhelming numbers, the Russians seemed to find the Japanese too much for them, and all at once discontinued the attack and disappeared in the darkness. But our brave Sugimura was severely wounded. A shot from a machine-gun went through his head. He did not succumb to the wound for some minutes, but continued to shout and encourage his men, until he saw, though his blood was fast running into his eyes, the enemy retreat!

The Russians left more than ten dead behind them. Early next morning, July 17, they came with a Red-Cross flag and stretchers, coolly approached our patrol line, coming as near as fifty metres, and trying to peep into our camp under the pretense of picking up their dead! This, as also their unwarranted use of the white flag and of our sun flag, was a despicable attempt at deceiving us. Not only once, but frequently, did they repeat these shabby tricks. One time they showed their meanness in another way. At one spot our sentinel noticed a dark shadow coming forward, so cried, as usual: —

"Halt! Who goes there?"

"Officer of our army —"

The Japanese patrol thought that a scouting officer had come back and said: "Pass on!" Suddenly the dark shadow attacked the sentinel with his bayonet. The latter, who was at once undeceived,

120

exclaimed: "You enemy! Impudent fellow! Come on!" and knocked him down with the stock of his rifle. The enemy learned a few Japanese words and tried to use them to deceive us. Because the Russians did not scruple to resort to such small, unmanly tricks, we had always to be very careful and vigilant.

Lieutenant Sugimura was picked up and carried to a barn, where his attendant, Fukumatsu Ito, nursed him as a mother would her sick child. The faithful Ito grew pale with anxiety and fatigue. With his eyes full of tears, he would comfort and nurse his master. It was a touching sight to see him so thoroughly devoted to Lieutenant Sugimura. When the latter was sent to a field hospital, Ito used to go to visit him whenever he had leisure, walking a great distance over a rough road. One day on my way back from the headquarters of the brigade, I noticed a soldier coming up the hill, panting under a heavy load on his shoulder. Coming nearer, I found it was Ito. I asked him: —

"How is Lieutenant Sugimura's wound?"

"Extremely bad, I am sorry to say. He does not understand anything to-day."

"Indeed! Sugimura must surely be grateful for your kind care."

At this word of praise, Ito dropped a few tears, and said: "I do regret that I was not wounded together with my lieutenant. I have not had time

肉
彈

enough to return his kindness to me, and now we must part, it seems to me. It would have been far better if we had died together. It was but last night that my lieutenant grasped my hand in his and said to me, 'I am very grateful to you.' I felt so sad then, and longed to die with my lieutenant."

I could not watch this faithful man's face any longer. He added, "I must hurry on and see him," and went on in a dejected state of mind. His heavy parcel was full of Sugimura's things.

Sugimura's sad wound incited all the officers and men to a greater determination to chastise the enemy on Taipo-shan in front of us; they were all anxious to avenge the death and wounding of so many of their comrades. Those who died on outpost duty were of course sorry not to give their lives on a more glorious battle-field. Some of their dying words were so full of indignation and regret that they reached the marrow of the hearer's bones. As one of the most characteristic instances of this kind I venture to introduce a soldier by the name of Heigo Yamashita. This man was always earnest and obedient in doing his duty and would never grudge any amount of toil. His comrades loved and respected him and regarded him as a model soldier. One day he turned to his best friend and said, most solemnly: —

"I never expect to go back alive. I have no other desire than that I be allowed to go and meet my

122

comrades who died ten years ago, and tell them that the vengeance is complete — but I have one elder brother who is living in poverty. When I die, please let him know how brilliantly my death-flower blossomed."

Not long after this, he was ordered to convey an important message; on his way back to report the successful discharge of his duty, he was shot through the abdomen, and cried out: "What of this? A mere trifle!" But he could stand no longer. He was carried to the first aid station; the surgeon who examined him shook his head sadly and said that the man could not be saved.

The colonel of his regiment paid a visit to this valiant soldier and comforted him, saying: "Don't lose hope! You suffer badly, but you must keep up your courage." But seeing that the man's end was fast approaching, the colonel's eyes were dim with tears, when he said: "It is a wound of honor! You have done well." At this kind word Heigo opened his eyes a little and squeezed this forcible entreaty out of his agony: "Colonel, please pardon me. — Pray avenge me."

His hand trembled, and his lips quivered as if he wished to say more; soon he started on the journey from which none return. Poor Heigo! he could not join the great fight soon to take place, but died in this sad way. An apology for not doing anything better and an entreaty to be avenged were the last

肉
弾

words of this loyal subject. On the following day his comrades interred his remains in the field, and Chaplain Toyama read prayers and gave him a posthumous name according to the Buddhist custom. The tomb-post bearing this new name was set up facing Port Arthur.[1]

Here I must tell you about a memorial service for the dead that was held in the camp. Since our attack on Kenzan, we had lost no small number of men, so his Excellency the Commander of our Division appointed the 1st of July for a service in memory of those brave souls. An altar was raised on a farm near Lingshwuihotszu toward the cloudy evening of that day. It was called an altar, but in reality it was only a desk that we found in a farmer's yard. It was covered with white cloth, and a picture of Amida Buddha that Chaplain Toyama happened to have was hung above it. In front of the altar, boxes were piled up containing the ashes, — these boxes were about five inches square. Also provision was made for burning incense, and the altar was set facing Port Arthur. The dim light of candles added to the gloom and sadness of the occasion; the insects singing far and near seemed to chant about the inconstancy of all things. A shower falling through the willow-branches, which were being combed by the winds, seemed like tears of heaven. The officers of the division formed a semicircle before the altar,

[1] To enable his spirit to see the fall of the fortress.

the soldiers stood behind them, and when the read-
ing of the Scriptures by the chaplain was ended, the
commander stepped forward solemnly and offered
incense, then bowed his head and did not raise it for
some minutes. His heart was full of untold grief
and gratitude. His lips were repeating the phrase,
"You have done well!" The spirits of the brave
dead must also have been grieved to have left such
a worthy general. Other officers, one by one, followed the general, bowing and offering incense,
each sorrowing over his unfortunate subordinates.
"You have fought bravely and proved the success
of my training. You have faithfully done your
duty and been useful instruments in the hands of
His Majesty," was the silent tribute each officer
gave his own men. The surviving men, who had
entered the garrison at the same time with those
unfortunate comrades and striven with them in the
performance of their daily duties, must have envied
their manly, heroic death and wished they had
so distinguished themselves as to die with them.
The drops moistening the sleeves of the officers and
men, now bowing before the altar, were not merely
from the shower of heaven.

第
十
六

THE BATTLE OF TAIPO–SHAN

AFTER we repulsed the enemy at Kenzan in
their desperate attempts at retaking the hill,
our position increased daily in strength. On the
one hand, every preparation was being made for
an aggressive movement. Twelve guns captured
at Nanshan were arranged on the heights near
Lwanni-chiao, and six heavy naval guns were placed
on the height to the west of Chuchin-antsu. On the
other hand, powerful scouting parties were being
frequently dispatched to ascertain the arrangement
of the advance posts of the enemy. At this time,
the enemy's main position was on the steep hills
between Eijoshi in the north with Shwangtai-kou
and Antsu-ling in the middle, and Taipo-shan and
Laotso-shan in the south. They had fortified these
naturally strong places with everything that money
and time could afford, fully determined not to allow
us Japanese to advance even one step south of this
line. So it was extremely difficult to take this position by storm. But we had been drawing our bow
for a month, and were now quite ready and anxious

to let the arrow go. The opportunity ripened, the men's morale was at its best. On July 26, all the columns and corps started from our position with one accord to descend upon the Russian position in the south.

The sole objective of the regiment to which I belonged was the strongly fortified Taipo-shan, on which the enemy relied as the most important point in their advance position. On the night previous to the opening of hostilities the plan of campaign was minutely explained to us; the brigadier-general specially urged officers and men to do their uttermost and never to stop until the place was captured, saying that this battle was the first important step toward the real investment of Port Arthur, and that we were to attack the strongest of the enemy's advance posts. Our colonel also addressed us, and said that this was the first time that our regiment was to fight as a whole; that the final victory of a battle is, in fact, won early in the struggle; that all our lives belonged to him as our commander and that he would not hesitate to sacrifice them, but would resort to whatever means he might think advisable, during the act of fighting. He also told us that this was the time for us to put to test the spirit of Bushidō,[1] in which we had been long and carefully

[1] The Japanese code of knightly honor. For further particulars see "Bushidō, or The Soul of Japan," by Inazo Nitobe, published by G. P. Putnam's Sons.

127

trained; that we must remember his every-day instructions in general and the one given on the day of our departure from the garrison in particular, so that we might concentrate our thoughts and aspirations upon justifying His Majesty's gracious trust in us, and be ready to fall, all of us, under the honored banner of our regiment. This was truly a solemn injunction! The commanders of the battalions and companies followed suit, and each of us was carefully put in mind of his duty and urged to do his very best to keep the honor of the regiment unsullied. Thus our already willing determination was made still firmer and stronger. We were in such an uplifted state of mind that we had taken the whole of Taipo-shan before beginning hostilities.

The scene in the camp presented an extraordinary sight during the night previous to our march. Comrade was whispering with comrade here and there. Some there were who grasped their rifles lightly and smiled a lonely smile by themselves. Others changed to their best and cleanest underwear, so that they might not disgrace themselves before the enemy, dead in dirty clothing. Still others were looking vacantly into the heavens and singing in an undertone. And what was I thinking at this moment? All, I hope, were equally anxious to be able to die happy and contented, saying, "I have done my duty, by the blessing of Heaven."

Before daybreak of the 26th of July, when the fog was so thick that we could not see a foot ahead, and a cool breeze was sweeping through space after the shower of the previous evening, thousands of warriors began to move like a long serpent through the dark. At 3 A. M. we reached the foot of Iwayama, which was assigned to the reserve of our regiment. On the top of this hill was the position for the skirmishers; another hill to the right was assigned to the artillery. Until the signal for opening hostilities was given, even one man's head was not allowed to be thrust out of the line. All loaded their guns and were breathlessly waiting for the colonel's order, "Fire!" He was standing on the top of Iwayama with his field-glasses in his hand; his aide-de-camp stood before him with an open map, and occasionally fumbled about in his knapsack. Pack-horses loaded with ammunition were gathered together at the foot of the hill, and the soldiers detailed to distribute it were eagerly waiting to begin work. The signal was to be a cannon-shot; we studied the hands of our watches and our hearts jumped as the time went on minute after minute.

At forty-nine minutes past seven, the first roar was at last heard on the left wing. It was the signal for commencing attack on the enemy along Laotso-shan and Taipo-shan. For the last twenty days, we had not discharged a single shot, so this cannon

肉
弾

report must have taken the enemy unawares, and their hurried response sounded dull and sleepy and went high above our heads. Our plan was that the left wing should first attack and defeat the enemy on Laotso-shan, and then our detachment was to reinforce it. So we had to remain idle for some time and watch the progress of their attack on Laotso-shan. After a while, our naval guns began to make such a tremendous noise, that we hoped the enemy would soon be scared to death and give up their advance posts as our easy prey. But they proved stronger than we thought and did not disperse themselves like baby-spiders before our assault.

The fight increased in severity as time went on; our whole artillery was concentrated upon the heavy artillery on the northern slope of Laotso-shan and endeavored with might and main to silence them. After some time, when the enemy's fire had slackened a little, our infantry of the left wing began to march forward under the protecting fire of our artillery. At once they captured a crescent-shaped height, about two thousand metres ahead of us; immediately afterward they turned to the left and occupied the northern shoulder of Laotso-shan at ten o'clock. It seemed that the Russians had not fortified these places very strongly, for, after some resistance, they gave up the large fort on the important spot of Laotso-shan. Still their resistance was quite stubborn, and even when our infantry occu-

pied the top of the hill, a portion of the enemy still
stuck to the southern slope and stood fearlessly and
desperately under our concentrated downward fire.
This was the cause of the long duration of this attack. Eventually our left wing succeeded in routing
and driving them away from this spot; but they
had the inlet of Lungwang-tang at their back and
could not retreat in that direction. Soon they were
hard pressed and obliged to leave many dead and
wounded behind; the remainder jumped into junks
and concealed themselves on the opposite side of
the inlet.

The work assigned to the left wing being thus
finished, our regiment now had the great opportunity of attacking the enemy. Whereupon Colonel
Aoki ordered all his captains, "Whole line begin
firing from the right." All at once the whole line
thrust out its head, the first and second battalions
on the right and the third on the left. Their firing
sounded like popping corn. As soon as we began,
the Russian bullets began to fall in large drops
about us, stirring up sand, kicking stones, and fell-
ing men. Those that passed near our ears made a
whistling sound, and those going high through the
air, a trembling boom. Our skirmish-line, forming
a long chain, lost its links here and there; the carriers of stretchers ran hither and thither conveying
the dead and wounded to the first aids. There was
not only the hail of rifle-shot, but large projectiles

第十六

131

began to burst over our heads and emit white smoke. The fragments of shell fell on the ground with a thud and made holes, or pierced the skirmishers' heads from above. Sometimes the empty case of a shell would go past the hill and fall in the midst of our reserve. While I was still with the reserve I actually saw a soldier, who was struck by such an empty shell, lose his right arm and die on the spot. When we examined an empty shell later on, we discovered inside it, first a piece of overcoat, then a piece of coat, then a piece of undershirt, then flesh and bone, then again underwear, coat, and overcoat, together with grass and pebbles stained with blood.

This struggle lasted for several hours; the enemy's artillery was very strong and we could not find a chance to go forward. Our dead and wounded increased so fast that the stretchers prepared were not sufficient. The fire reached even the first aid stations far in the rear. Some wounded soldiers there were injured again or killed. It was a desperate fight. The reserves were brought about to the left of the artillery's position, so that they could form an assaulting column at a moment's notice and rush upon the enemy when the opportunity came. At this time I was with them, carrying the regimental flag. Because our position was with the artillery and because the flag was a great target for the enemy, the Russians in Wangchia-tun began at once

a fierce fire on us. Their concentrated fire was well
aimed, and their shells came like rain, falling side-
ways in the wind. When the smoke cleared away
for a minute, we found a lieutenant who had, just a
moment before, been bravely ordering his men, lying
dead covered with blood. The chief of the gun detachment and also the gunners were torn to pieces,
their brains gushing out and their bowels mixing
with mud and blood. When the reserve gunners
went to take their places, they also were killed.
Such a bloody scene can never be realized without
an actual sight; my pen is powerless to describe it.

Our reserve having suffered no small loss before
the strong fire of the enemy, we had no resource
left but to try a desperate assault upon them. Every
moment longer that we remained in this position
meant the loss of so many more men. Clouds had
been gathering and lowering in the sky for some
time; it was dark and dreary. Soon the swift wind
ran side by side with powder and smoke, and muddy
rain fell obliquely with the shot and shell. At this
dismal stage of affairs we, the reserves, were ordered
to join the colonel. We at once left the artillery and
began to march to the left, clambering over the
rocks. The sharp wind flapped the colors violently, and I feared that they might be torn to
pieces any moment. At this juncture a shell burst
over my head and its fragments rent the air; a part
of the flag was blown away, a man was killed,

肉
弾

and a piece of the shell fell into a valley far behind us.

As was said before, the colonel was on the top of Iwayama; the enemy was sure that our strength was concentrated there and showered upon it a hailstorm of shrapnel. Colonel Aoki stood in the midst of that as firm and unflinching as Ni-ō or Fudō,[1] staring at the enemy with steady gaze. When I approached him and reported the tearing of the flag, he simply remarked, "So!" After a while he said, "Is n't this just like a manœuvre?"

He was so full of courage and strength, his fearless and composed attitude was such an inspiration to his subordinates, that the somewhat despondent soldiers at once recovered their spirits and energy on looking up at his face.

It was already 2 P. M., and yet the fighting had not come to any decisive result. Our casualties increased in number hour after hour. At this moment a portion of our left wing began to move forward. Our detachment was also ordered forward, whereupon the whole line of men rose like a dark fence, and pushed on right to the muzzles of the enemy's guns. The Russians seized this opportunity to increase the intensity of their fire; those of us who

[1] Ni-ō, the two kings, Indra and Brahma, who keep guard at the gateways of Buddhist temples, to scare away demons. They are noted for their grimness of expression. Fudō, the "Immovable," the God of Wisdom, who is represented of stern expression, and surrounded by a halo of flames.

went forward were mowed down, and those who did
not press on were already dead! Lieutenant Yatsuda was shot through the chest, yet he continued
to shout, "Forward! Forward!" paying no attention to the gushing blood and without letting his men
know of his wound. He pressed on furiously about
a thousand metres toward the enemy, and when he
approached the line to be occupied he shouted Banzai faintly and died.

A brave commander's men are always brave! One
of Yatsuda's men had his right arm shattered before his lieutenant was shot, but he would not stay
behind. When the lieutenant told him to go to the
first aid, he said, "Why, such a tiny wound! I can
still fight very well, sir." He poured out water from
his bottle and washed his wound, bound it up with a
Japanese towel, and pressed on panting with the
skirmishers, his gun in his left hand. When he came
near the enemy's line, he was killed by the side of
Lieutenant Yatsuda, whom the brave fellow considered his elder brother. Even in his death he
grasped his gun firmly. Both of them showed the
true spirit of Japanese warriors, doing their duty
till the last moment and even after death.

At last the reserve in the hands of Colonel Aoki
was reduced to two companies of infantry and one
of engineers. What a disastrous struggle this had
been! Ever since morning our artillery had been trying hard to silence the powerful guns of the enemy.

第十六

Their desperate efforts were all in vain, and the strong posts of the enemy remained without damage. What a disappointment! Our infantry were already only five or six hundred metres from the enemy, but until our artillery should have destroyed the offensive and defensive works of the Russian forts, an assault would have resulted only in complete annihilation. So these infantry men were patiently waiting quite close to the enemy for the right moment to come. The long summer day at last came to its close, and the dreary curtain of darkness enveloped the scene of battle.

The rain ceased for a while, but the night was dismal. Hundreds of dead bodies were strewn on hill and in valley, while the enemy's forts towered high against the dark sky as if challenging us to a fruitless attack. But our morale was not at all impaired; on the contrary, this day's failure added to our firm resolve to storm and defeat the Russians on the next. During the night the firing of guns and rifles went on unceasingly, and in carrying the dead we had to use tents to supply the deficiency of stretchers. The wounded were also picked up and carried to the rear by the ambulance men. And we who had escaped injury sat by the side of our silent dead and without sleep waited impatiently for a better day to break.

第
十
七

THE OCCUPATION OF TAIPO-SHAN

O N the next day, the 27th, fully determined to drive out the enemy, our entire artillery began firing at early dawn, striving to open a passage for our infantry. Our bombardment was more violent than on the previous day, and the enemy's response was also proportionately fiercer. Why was it that the Russian forts were so strangely impregnable? On the line connecting the heights their trenches were faced with rocks and covered with timber roofs, and they could fire at us through portholes, safely concealed and protected from our bursting shells. They had quick-firing guns and machine-guns arranged in different places so that they could fire at us from all points and directions, and these formidable guns were well protected with strong works built of strong material. Added to all this, the side of our hill and the opposite side of their hill formed a rocky valley with almost perpendicular walls, so that we could not climb down or up without superhuman efforts. To attack such a strongly armed enemy in a place of such natural

137

advantage meant a great amount of sacrifice on our part.

So long as our artillery remained unsuccessful, our rifle fire was of course of no use. Somehow we must damage the enemy's machine-guns, otherwise all our efforts would end only in adding to our already long list of dead and wounded. This we well understood, but if we could not utilize our firearms, our only and last resource was to shoot off human beings, to attack with bullets of human flesh. With such unique weapons, — human bullets, the consolidated essence of Yamato Damashii, — how could we fail to rout the enemy? Orders were soon given. The fifth, seventh, and tenth companies of our regiment precipitated themselves down into the valley and began a furious assault on the enemy; whereupon the Russian artillery, who had hitherto been aiming at our artillery, directed their guns upon this forlorn hope, this rushing column. Simultaneously all the machine-guns and all the infantry in the forts concentrated their fire upon this desperate body, who pressed on like a swift wind with shouts and yells, not a whit daunted by this devilish fire. Their shrieks and the cannon-roar combined sounded like a hundred thunders thundering at the same moment. Press on! rush in! They fought like so many furies, wounded officers unheeded and fallen comrades ignored! Stepping on and jumping over the dead and dying, the survivors came at

last within a dozen metres or so of the enemy. But
they could not overcome nature — the rocky precipice stood like a screen before them, and half their
comrades were strewn dead on the side of the hill
at their backs; they could do nothing but stand
there facing and staring at the enemy. While this
assaulting column was pressing on under the heavy
shower of shells and bullets, the sight was stirring
beyond words; the men moved on like light gray
shadows enshrouded in volumes of smoke. Some of
them were seen flying high up in the air, hurled by
the big shells. When their bodies were picked up,
some had no wound at all, but the skin had turned
purplish all over. This was caused by the throwing
up and consequent heavy fall on the ground.

The enemy's resistance was so stubborn that our
fire seemed as powerless as beating a big temple-
bell with a pin. If we had gone on in this way, we
might have failed entirely. We had to attempt a
final charge at the risk of annihilation. Soon the following order was given by the brigadier-general: —

"The courageous behavior of our officers and
men since the beginning of the battle is worthy of all
admiration. Our brigade is to attack the enemy
along the eastern side of Taipo-shan at 5 P. M. to-
day, to bombard with the entire force of the artillery,
and the left wing to charge when our bombardment
opens to them an opportunity, and thus to over-
whelm and defeat the enemy. Your regiment must

139

肉
弾

strive with the utmost effort to improve this opportunity and occupy the enemy's position at your
front."

Yes, we were anxious to defeat the enemy with
our utmost and most desperate effort! This was the
day for us to unfurl our colors high above the enemy's fortress and to comfort the spirits of those who
during the past few days had died without hearing
a triumphant Banzai.

A group of officers, while waiting for a proper
opportunity to strike, were talking about the condition of affairs since the previous morning.

"The enemy is certainly brave! I noticed a Russian officer commanding his men from the top of a
breastwork."

"Yes, they are fighting hard; but we must carry
their position *to-day!*"

We were beginning to feel that the Russian strength
came not only from their mechanical defenses, but
also from their intrepid behavior; but all were
agreed in their ardent resolve to defeat the enemy
and avenge their unfortunate comrades. Presently
a young officer came along with a bottle of beer.
Since the previous day we had been almost without food or drink, and this bottle of beer seemed a
strange sight on the battle-field. We all wondered
who he might be, and as he drew nearer we recognized Lieutenant Kwan, adjutant of the battalion.

"Isn't it a rare treat, this beer? I have been

carrying this bottle in my belt since yesterday, to drink a Banzai in the enemy's position. But now let us drink it together as a farewell cup. You have all been very kind to me — I have made up my mind to die beautifully to-day."

The young officer talked very cheerily and yet in real earnest, and filled his aluminum cup with the golden beverage. The cup went round among the group, and we smiled a melancholy smile over the drink. This ceremony over, Lieutenant Kwan raised the empty bottle high in the air and shouted, "I pray for your health!" and ran away to bury the dead. How could we know that this was his true farewell? Soon afterwards, without waiting for the happy moment of shouting Banzai in the enemy's position, he joined the ranks of the illustrious dead. He and I came from the same province and we were very old and intimate friends; he loved me as his younger brother. So, every time we met on the battle-field, we used to grasp each other's hand with fervor and say, "Are you all right?" Even such an exchange of words was an occasion of great pleasure to us. At this meeting, not knowing of course that it was the last time I was to see him, I failed to thank him for all his past friendship toward me. We had such a hurried, unsatisfactory, eternal good-by, as is usual on the battle-field. I learned afterward that the lieutenant, while superintending the burial of the dead, said to his men: "Please cover them

141

肉
彈

carefully with earth, because I myself am to be treated in the same way very soon."

Was he really conscious of his impending death? Lieutenant Yatsuda also, who died earlier than Kwan, suddenly pulled out a packet of dry chest-nuts[1] from his pocket during his advance and said to his servant: "This was offered to the gods by my mother, and she told me to eat this without fail before fighting. I will eat one and you also eat one. This may be our last farewell!"

They bowed politely and munched the hard nuts together! Of course we were all ready for death, and each time we met we thought was the last. But when the true moment comes, some mysterious, invisible wire seems to bring the sad message to the heart.

It was 5 P. M. Our whole artillery opened fire at the same time, and the whole force of infantry also joined in the bombardment. Heaven and earth at once became dark with clouds of smoke, and the war of flying balls and exploding shells threatened to rend mountain and valley. This was meant to be the decisive battle, so its violence and fury were beyond description. Our infantry shot and advanced, stopped and shot, rushing on and jumping forward. The hail-storm of the enemy's projectiles did not allow them to march straight on. Sometimes "Lieu-

[1] *Kachi-guri*, dry chestnuts. The word *kachi* also means victory, hence it is one of the articles given to a departing soldier as a wish for his success.

tenant" was the last faint word of gratitude from a
dying man. Again "A-a!" was the only sound made
by the expiring soldier. But this was not the moment to take notice of these sickening scenes; we
had to press on if it were only an inch nearer the
enemy. What did the brigadier-general say in his
message? "I admire your bravery," were the words.
Did he not say, "strive with your utmost effort"?
Forward! march! advance! and be killed! This was
not the time to stop for even half a moment! Such
was the thought, and such were the words of encouragement from the officers, who ran about right
and left on the battle-line, brandishing their drawn
swords, stirring up their men and inspiring them
with invincible spirit. Two companies of reserves
and reserve engineers were also sent to the first line.
At last our First Battalion came within twenty metres
of the enemy, but the screen-like rocky hill on which
there was hardly any foothold still stood before
them. Desperately anxious to climb up, yet utterly
unable to do so while the shower of the enemy's
bullets swept them from the side, the Second Company facing the enemy's front became a mere target for the Russians' machine-guns and was mowed
down in a few brief moments. One bullet went
through the sword blade and slightly injured the left
eye of Captain Matsumaru. Our artillery fire made
a pyrotechnic display in the air, but did hardly any
damage to the enemy's defensive constructions.

Shrapnel was of no avail: we had to explode spherical shells, and smash the covering of the enemy's trenches. "Even at the risk of damage to our own infantry, fire spherical shells as rapidly as possible," was the message repeatedly sent to the artillery, but no single orderly came back alive: all were killed before reaching their destination. The lieutenant of the engineers was ordered to send explosives, but this also could not be done in time.

Seven o'clock had passed, eight o'clock too, and it was now nine, but there was no improvement in our condition. The First Battalion was obliged to halt for a while. The commander of the Second Battalion, Major Temai, was seriously wounded; the adjutant, while reconnoitring a route for the assault, was shot through the head and died as he turned and said, "Report!" The Third Battalion came close to the enemy, but could do nothing more: its dead and wounded increased moment after moment. Our situation was just like that of a small fish about to be swallowed by a huge whale, — we could not improve it by our own efforts. However, such was the tenacity of purpose and invincible courage pervading our ranks, that our determination and resourcefulness became greater as the enemy proved more difficult to subdue. All the battalions, more particularly the First, were now breaking rocks with picks and piling up stones to make footholds. But the work was not easy, so near the enemy that both

144

parties were like two tigers showing their teeth and threatening to tear each other to pieces. The Russians tried hard to hinder our work; the slightest sound of a pick would immediately invite a tongue of fire that licked the place around us ravenously. In the midst of this great difficulty, a sort of foothold was made at last, and now we were ready to push in with one accord!

The night was growing old; a dismal waning moon was shining dimly over the battle-ground, showing one half of our camp in a light black-and-white picture. Major Uchino, commander of the Second Battalion, sent the following message to our colonel:

"Our battalion is about to try an assault, expecting its own annihilation. I hope that you also will assume the offensive. I sincerely hope and believe that my most revered and beloved colonel will be the successful commander of the attack, and that by the time the sun rises our honored regimental flag may fly over the enemy's parapets. I hereby offer my respects and farewell to you."

Then we heard the solemn tune of "Kimi ga yo" sounded by trumpets far away at the left wing. The moon shone through the small sky of our valley, and the long-drawn faint echo of the national air seemed to penetrate our hearts. The music sounded to us as if His Majesty were ordering us forward in person. The officers and men straightened themselves up, leaped and bounded with overwhelming courage,

145

all at once burst over the enemy's breastworks with shouts and yells, braving the shower of fire and clambering over the rocks and stones. Major Matsumura, at the head of the foremost group of men, shouted with stirring and flaming eyes: "Charge! forward!" The music swelled still more inspiringly, and all the succeeding bands of men shouted Banzai with an earth-shaking voice and encouraged their onrushing comrades. At the top of the hill the clash of bayonets scattered sparks — hand-to-hand conflict at close quarters was the last effort, the impact of the human bullets, the sons of Yamato. "You haughty land-grabbers, see now the folly of your policy," was the idea with which every man struck his blow, the consequence being a stream of blood and a hill of corpses. It was a hard struggle, but at the same time it was a great joy to defeat the enemy after repeated failures! Body after body of men rushed in like waves — the Russians found it altogether too much for them. They wavered and yet continued for some time longer to resist us in close hand-to-hand fight, while we increased in courage and strength in proportion to their diminution of power. At last, at 8 A. M. of July 28, when the eastern sky was crimson, we became the undisputed masters of the heights of Taipo-shan.

The imperial colors waved high above our new camp, and the Banzai of rejoicing arose like surges of the sea!

146

第
十
八

THE FIELD AFTER THE BATTLE

BEFORE we at last secured the enemy's position along the heights of Taipo-shan, all of us, from the division commander to the lowest soldier, had exerted our perseverance and bravery to the uttermost. We had fought against an enemy having a position naturally advantageous and strongly fortified; we had fought for fifty-eight hours without food, drink, or sleep, against a desperately stubborn foe. Our final success was pregnant of many important results to the subsequent plan of campaign. The battle of Nanshan, with more than four thousand casualties, had been considered the hardest of struggles so far; but, compared with Taipo-shan, Nanshan was won at a low cost. At Nanshan the enemy had an extended slope before them, where they swept away our attacking forces from a secure position. The nature of the ground along Taipo-shan was totally different, built up with perpendicular hills and deep valleys. We could defend ourselves in a dead angle, or could conceal and cover ourselves easily. And yet our casualties here amounted to the same number as at Nanshan. You can judge from this fact how severe was the battle.

For three days we contended for a small space of ground; no food at all could be conveyed from the rear. We only munched hard biscuits, our "iron rations," could not dip with one hand a drop of water to drink, and did not sleep even a moment. But because we were so excited and anxious and determined, no thought occurred to us of being sleepy or hungry. The Russians also were in a similar condition. When we examined their skirmish-trenches, after our occupation of the place, we found them full of nastiness; the men must have remained there without moving one step for the long fifty-eight hours. The only difference was that they had no difficulty in the way of provisions, for our men were made happy with the black bread, lump-sugar, etc., that the enemy had left behind.

The first thing we felt when our work was done was sleepiness! We desired nothing but sleep. Groups here and there, talking about their dead comrades and their experiences, soon began to nod, one man after another, and would lie down under the coverings of the enemy's trenches in a most innocent, childlike manner. The Russian dead scattered all about, weltering in blood, did not disturb their profound sleep. Neither did they think of eating or drinking; their snores sounded like distant thunder. Occasional bullets of the enemy did not disturb them even as much as the humming of mosquitoes.

The sublimity of a battle can only be seen in the midst of showers of bullet and shell, but the dismal horror of it can best be observed when the actual struggle is over. The shadow of impartial Death visits friend and foe alike. When the shocking massacre is over, countless corpses covered with blood lie long and flat in the grass and between stones. What a deep philosophy their cold faces tell! When we saw the dead at Nanshan, we could not help covering our eyes in horror and disgust. But the scene here, though equally shocking, did not make us shudder half so much. Some were crushed in head and face, their brains mixing with dust and earth. The intestines of others were torn out and blood was trickling from them. The sight of these things, however, did not horrify us very much. At Nanshan we did not actually fight, but only visited the scene afterward. This time we were accustomed to these sights through the long hours of suffering and desperate struggle.

At Nanshan, with the enemy's dead in front of us, we could not but sympathize with and pity them; but here we hated and loathed them. How were they to blame? Were not they also warriors who died in the discharge of their duty? But after a hard struggle with them, in which we had had to sacrifice the lives of so many of our beloved men, our hearts involuntarily hated our opponents, who we wished had yielded to us more easily, but who resisted us to their utmost — and butchered our men from their secure trenches, thrusting out their guns from the holes. Of course our reason does not sanction it, but those who have had experience in actual fighting will easily sympathize with this sense of hatred and indignation at the sight of the dead of a brave but stubborn foe. Of course it is a silly thing, and we do all admire without stint their valor and perseverance. Their success in keeping us at bay for fifty-eight hours, under our overwhelming attack, is certainly worthy of a great military power. One Russian was found dead in a skirmish-trench with his head bandaged. Probably he fought on bravely in spite of his first wound until a second shot from our side gave him his death-blow. Those Russian dead, scattered in front of their breastworks, must have been the brave ones who rushed out of their trenches when we burst in, and fought us with their bayonets and fists. Some had photographs of their wives and children in their bosoms, and these pictures were bespattered with blood. One inclined so to do may condemn it as effeminate and weak to carry such things into battle; but thousands of miles away from home, at the dismal and bloody seat of war, where they could not hear from their beloved ones, was it not natural for them to yearn after them deep down in their hearts and console themselves with the sight of these pictures? It is human nature that every new landscape, every new phase of the moon, makes one think of home and friends — and brave fighters are also human, are they not?

> "The bravest is the tenderest,
> The loving are the daring."

Are not these the poet's words? Those poor Russian soldiers, hunted out to the battle-field by the fury of oppression, had to suffer and die far away from home. Their situation deserves nothing but commiseration and sympathy!

As soon as the battle was over, my servant came to me with a hold-all left by the Russians. We opened it and found it full of all kinds of things, and among them a suit of Chinese clothes. This latter item was a surprise to us, and also an explanation. We had seen Russian scouts in Chinese costume who had appeared within our picket-line, and now at last we had found out their secret. They were certainly clever in the trick of quickly changing costume and character as if on the stage. During the War of American Independence, the English sentries were killed almost nightly by the enemy clad in goat-skins. Had the Russians learned the art from the Americans? They tried every trick in scouting — it was not only the real Russians who undertook this work, but even ghosts and appari-

肉
彈

tions were invited to join. We found also Japanese flags that they had left; perhaps they had even tried to deceive us with our own colors.

After this battle we captured some damaged machine-guns; this was the firearm most dreaded by us. A large iron plate serves the purpose of a shield, through which aim is taken, and the trigger can be pulled while the gun is moving upward, downward, to the left, or to the right. More than six hundred bullets are pushed out automatically in one minute, as if a long, continuous rod of balls was being thrown out of the gun. It can also be made to sprinkle its shot as roads are watered with a hose. It can cover a larger or smaller space, or fire to a greater or less distance as the gunner wills. Therefore, if one becomes the target of this terrible engine of destruction, three or four shot may go through the same place in rapid succession, making the wound very large. The bullets are of the same size as those used in rifles. A large number of these shot are inserted in a long canvas belt — and this belt is loaded into the chamber of the gun; it works like the film of the vitascope. And the sound it makes! Heard close by, it is a rapid succession of tap, tap, tap; but from a distance it sounds like a power loom heard late at night when everything else is hushed. It is a sickening, horrible sound! The Russians regarded this machine-gun as their best friend, and certainly it did very much as a means of defense.

They were wonderfully clever in the use of this machine. They would wait till our men came very near them, four or five *ken* only, and just at the moment when we proposed to shout a triumphant Banzai, this dreadful machine would begin to sweep over us as if with the besom of destruction, the result being hills and mounds of dead. After this battle of Taipo-shan we discovered in the enemy's position the body of one soldier called Hyodo, who had been one of the forlorn-hope scouts of the Second Company. He had no less than forty-seven shot in his body, twenty-five on the right arm only. Another soldier of a neighboring regiment received more than seventy shot. These instances prove how destructive is the machine-gun! Of course, the surgeons could not locate so many wounds in one body, and they invented a new name, "Whole body honeycombed with gun-wounds." Whenever our army attacked the enemy's position, it was invariably this machine-gun that made us suffer and damaged us most severely.

In this camp we found four or five of the enemy's war-dogs dead. They were strongly built, with short brown hair and sharp clever faces. They were shot by our guns, and, though brutes, had participated in the honorable death of the battle-field. The Russians train these dogs for war purposes and make them useful in more ways than one. I am told that sometimes these dogs acted as scouts.

I carefully inspected the scene of this terrible

肉
彈
fight and learned how strong were both the natural position and the arrangements for defense. I almost marveled at our final success, even with a terrible loss of life and blood. Our engineers dug out a number of ground-mines and destroyed wire-entanglements put up by the enemy. The Russian loss was also very severe; a large number of their dead were left in the camp or on the line of their retreat—those whom they with difficulty picked up, were piled upon ten or more ox-carts and carried away through Hanchia-tun toward Port Arthur.

Let me leave the battle-field for a while and tell you what impression our army gave the Russians, and also recount the story of one or two valiant soldiers. After this battle, our detachment picked up a note written by the commander of a Russian division. Translated, it is as follows:—

"The Japanese army knows how to march, but not how to retreat. Once they begin to attack a position, they continue most fiercely and most obstinately. That I can approve of, but when circumstances do not permit a forward march, a retreat may sometimes be made useful. But the Japanese always continue an attack irrespective of the amount of danger. Probably the Japanese books of tactics make no study at all of retreating."

Is ours a mere "wild-boar" courage, not to know how to retreat? "Back-roving" (*sakaro*) was ridiculed by the old warriors of Japan — our modern

154

fighters also despise the idea of retreating. It may be a mistake, but "to show one's back to the enemy" has always been considered the greatest disgrace a *samurai* could bring upon himself. This idea is the central military principle of the people of Japan. This note of the Russian general is good testimony to the spirit pervading our ranks, "determined to death" and to fight on with strenuous perseverance. Every time we fought we won, because we did not believe in retreating. The Russians, who were taught to believe that a retreat may sometimes be made useful, and who often boasted of their "masterly retreats," do not seem to have gained many victories by their skill in falling back.

To illustrate the truth of the Russian general's statement as to the spirit and determination of our men, I will recount here one or two instances. On the 27th one Sukeichi Matsumoto, assigned to the duty of a scout, braved the storm of fire and encouraged his comrades, always at the head of the little group and pressing on hard. Just after the dawn of that day he noticed blood trickling down his face, upon which he cried, "I'm done for!" He repeated the exclamation several times in succession and then fell. His corporal ran to the spot, raised him, and cried: "Keep up your spirits, my man!" Upon which Sukeichi opened his eyes, grasped the corporal's hand, and said, with a smile: "Why! I'm all right! Please march on!" Scarcely had the words escaped from his lips when he breathed his last.

There was a particularly brave sergeant called Semba in the Eighth Company. In the battle of Kenzan he distinguished himself by rushing in before others upon the enemy. He was used to march on, crying all the time, "*I* will avenge you, depend upon it!" thus comforting the dying or wounded who lay along his way. This he meant as an eternal farewell or a healing word as the case might be. So his subordinates loved him as their elder brother and thought they would be perfectly satisfied if they could die with Sergeant Semba. His lieutenant especially loved this sergeant and believed him to be better than a hundred ordinary men. For all difficult duties, he singled out this Semba, whose efforts were usually successful because of his composure and bravery. On the 27th, when the desperate march was set afoot, the sergeant held his men firmly together and pressed on headlong, crying, as usual, "*I* will avenge you, depend upon it!" to those falling right and left. At last he himself fell at the feet of his lieutenant, who tried to raise him and felt warm blood running over his hands. "I'm done for!" said the sergeant, faintly. "Keep up your spirits, Sergeant Semba!" The brave fellow spat out the blood that was filling his throat and with his eyes full of tears said: "Lieutenant! Port Arthur —" Without finishing his sentence he ex·

156

pired. Did he mean to say that he regretted dying before the final assault on Port Arthur? Or did he pray with tears that that fortress might fall into our hands as quickly as possible? Whatever it might be, one thing is certain, that this true patriot thought of nothing but Port Arthur in the moment of his death!

第十九

THE FIRST AID STATION

SINCE the opening of hostilities on the heights to the northeast of Hwangni-chuan and Ta-shang-tun, I had been too excited over the fighting to think of anything else, but now I began to think of my friend, Surgeon Yasui, and to wonder whether he had passed through the struggle in safety. On the eve of the 28th, when threatening clouds were gathering in the sky, I was walking alone under the willow trees along a small stream below Taipo-shan, by which we had bivouacked. As I was thinking that he must be extremely busy taking care of the wounded, suddenly I heard the clicking sound of an officer's boots, and he stood beside me.

"Dr. Yasui!"

"Lieutenant Sakurai!"

"Are you quite well?"

We shook hands heartily and, after commenting upon each other's emaciated appearance, discussed the severity and horror of the recent fight. Captain Matsumaru, who had been wounded, also came along, shouldering his sword, which had been bent out of shape by the shot that had opened a round window in its blade. He too joined earnestly in our conversation about the recent battle. From Surgeon Yasui we obtained a minute description of the sad and horrible scenes at the first aid station.

During the battle the enemy's shot fell constantly in the vicinity of the native dwellings, and in our temporary bandaging station the danger was very great. One time a big shell came through the roof and exploded in the courtyard, and a large number of the wounded men in the house were blown to pieces, the walls and pillars were spotted with blood and flesh; a shocking sight it was. On another occasion, just as the stretcher-bearers had brought in a wounded soldier from the battle-line with great difficulty, and put him down in the yard, an enemy's shot came flying and killed the poor man on the spot. These unfortunate fellows had fought valiantly on the battle-line, and had been picked up and carried back with wounds of honor, only to be killed in such a miserable way. The enemy's projectiles followed our brave men everywhere and killed them without mercy.

The dreary heartrending scene at the first aid is utterly beyond description. One cannot help associating it with the horrors of hell. As soon as a wounded man is carried back, be he officer or private, surgeons and hospital orderlies give him the

肉
弾

necessary first aid. As the firing on the battle-line increases in intensity, the number of the wounded increases faster and faster, and the surgeons and others have more than they can do. While attending one man, they notice perhaps that another man begins to breathe hard and lose his color. While giving a few drops of brandy to the second man, a third man may be expiring without any medical aid. Hardly have they had time to dress one man's wound properly, when ten or fifteen new ones are brought in. The surgeons are surrounded right and left by fatally wounded men. They work hard in their shirt sleeves, their whole attire covered with blood. Some men are bandaged, and others with broken limbs are helped by a splint. Of course all is done hurriedly and is only a temporary aid, but they are kept so busy, and the whole scene is so sad and urgent, that they feel as if they were losing their minds every moment, so much have they on their hands and so little can they actually do.

But those lying in this house or that yard are all brave soldiers. They would not grumble even if medical care were slow in coming, or insufficient when it came. They show no discontent, they have no special desires. Because the heat and excitement of the battle-field is still with them, they want to rush to the first line once more, whenever they hear the yell of fighters or the boom of guns. The surgeons try hard to pacify them and keep them still. Those made insane by wounds in the head raise faint cries of "Tenno Heika Banzai" [1] or of "Rusky," and stagger about. If a surgeon holds them fast, they angrily rebuke him, saying, "You Rusky!" The result of these frantic movements is generally an abundant loss of blood, soon followed by fainting and death.

On the 27th there was a specially large number of wounded. The farmyard in front of the first aid station was filled with the suffering from one end to the other. While a surgeon is taking care of one, some one behind pulls him by his trousers. On looking back, he finds a man leaning against him and like an innocent baby falling into the sleep that knows no awakening. "Mine is a life that cannot be saved, please kill me at once." So shouts a man in agony, clutching a surgeon with both hands. One sergeant crept on his hands, dragging his legs to the side of a surgeon. "Please, surgeon, the man over there is one of my company; he breathes so hard that it may be of no use, but please see him once more." This entreaty was accompanied by tears of sympathy. This kind sergeant was seriously injured, but his love of his subordinate made him brave and gallant. There were many also who themselves were on the brink of the grave, and yet who insisted on their comrades being first attended to, saying that they could well afford to wait. What

[1] "Ten thousand years for His Majesty the Emperor!"

161

noble self-denial! The brave men, though panting and gasping, with livid faces and blood-covered bodies, kept the true spirit of Bushido, which could not be soiled with the dust of battle, nor did they lose it with their heart's blood.

On the morning of the 27th a private came to the first aid station with a distracted, hollow countenance. A surgeon who noticed him asked, "What is the matter with you? Wounded?" No answer came from him, his lips moved in vain. The surgeon asked again, "What is it? I cannot know if you do not tell." Still no answer was forthcoming. The surgeon thought it very strange, and while gazing at the man's face he noticed a little blood on it. On closer examination it was found that this man had been shot through the temple from right to left, so that he had lost both sight and hearing. No sooner did the surgeon discover this than he began to attend to his case. But when he tenderly took the poor man's hand, the soldier grated his teeth and muttered "Revenge." His body stiffened very rapidly and he soon breathed his last. Poor brave fellow, he did not know he was dying, but was only anxious to fight again.

Here is another case. A wounded private came rushing into the station, swinging both arms as if in great haste. "It is a hot fight, extremely interesting! We shall occupy the place very soon." The surgeon asked him, "Are you wounded?" "A little at the

162

waist," was the answer. As the surgeon was very anxious about the issue of the day, he asked the man: "Have you killed many of the enemy? Which side has more casualties?" The man lowered his voice and said, "Once again, there are more casualties on Japan's side."

Then the surgeon examined his "little wound" about the waist and was astonished at the seriousness of the case. The flesh of the right hip had been entirely swept away by a shell. He was so proud of his bravery in action and faithful discharge of duty, that he did not know that drop by drop his very life was ebbing away. He talked about the battle cheerfully and in high spirits. "All right! Your bandaging is finished. You may go." At this word from the surgeon the man stood on his legs, but could not walk a step. The fever of war makes it possible for a man to walk and even run in such a condition. But once brought in by the bearers his nerves relax and he begins to feel the pain all at once. There have been many instances of this, and I was one of the number. I did not feel any pain at all during the two days I was lying on the field, but oh! the pain I began to feel when I was taken to the first aid and bandaged; the agony I then felt was so great that I wished I had died on the field. "To come to life from death," was certainly my own case, but I could not at all appreciate my rare good fortune at that time. I thought that Heaven was cruel not to have

第
十
九

163

killed me at once, instead of leaving me to suffer pain harder than death itself, in a state half dead and half alive.

While the fighting is yet going on the Red-Cross flags here and there beckon to those who are wounded in the field. The brave men who die on the spot receive no benefit from the great charity, but the wounded receive and monopolize its benefits, and sometimes feel as if they were stealing something from the worthy dead. As soon as a battle begins, the stretcher-carriers go about the field with stretchers on their shoulders, pick up the wounded at the front, and carry them to the first aid. These coolies — or carriers — must also be as brave and earnest as real combatants, else they could not do their work in an extremely dangerous place and moment. They are intrusted with the philanthropic and perilous business of braving sword and shot, searching out the wounded and carrying them to a safe place. They must share their scanty food and precious water with their patients, and must take every possible care of them and comfort and cheer them with loving hearts. The stretcher-bearer's hard toil and noble work deserve our unbounded gratitude.

The sick and wounded who are sent back to the hospitals at home are clad in white and given the kind and faithful nursing and comforting of the surgeons and women nurses. I myself am one of those who received their care with tears of gratitude. In a

164

home hospital everything is kindness and sympathy, but how is it at the front? In the summer, when I took part in actual engagements, large armies of flies attacked the wretched patients, worms would grow in the mouth or nose, and some of them could not drive the vermin away because their arms were useless. Hospital orderlies would fain have helped these poor sufferers, but their number was so small that there was only one of them to a hundred of the wounded. And the patients were exposed to the scorching sun in the day and to the rain or dew of the night, without covering. Sometimes the patients, after lying long on the field, were in an indescribable condition, and it was necessary to soak them in a stream and scrub them with a broom before dressing their wounds. These horrors were solely due to an unexpectedly large number of casualties produced by the unforeseen severity of the fighting. Those in charge of the surgical work were eager to take care of all as quickly as possible, and send them back to be healed and made ready to rejoin the ranks of the combatants as soon as possible; but as they had to crowd more than a thousand patients into a field hospital provided for two hundred, they were powerless to give any better care to the sufferers.

第二十

FOLLOWING UP THE VICTORY

WHEN the forts of Taipo-shan, made almost impregnable by nature, were at last taken by the Japanese forces, the proud Russians must have realized that they had no despicable foe in us. But because they had behind them the main line of defense surrounding the formidable fortress, they did not lose their courage with two or three defeats. So now they fell back upon the Kanta-shan Heights to construct new works of defense and try a third stand there. Because they were hurrying with this defensive construction, we too had to hurry with our attack. One day's delay on our part would give them a day's advantage over us. So without waiting to rest our tired backs and limbs after the long assault, we began a sustained pursuit with the force of a tidal wave, with a view to driving them to the main fortress while their defenses were as yet inadequate.

The 29th was spent in supplying the deficiency of ammunition, in the rearrangement of companies and ranks, and in a reconnaissance of the enemy's

166

cavalry. The following day, the 30th, was assigned for the simultaneous march of all our forces.

Our regiment put up a temporary bivouac in the valley near Hanchia-tun on the 29th. About three o'clock in the morning the brigade headquarters ordered our colonel to send for instructions at once. I was detailed for this duty and, accompanied by an orderly, ran one and one half *ri* along the river bank, and reached headquarters a little before four o'clock. Unless we ran still faster back to our camp, our regiment could not join the fight in time. So I took off all my clothing and handed it over to the orderly, and ran for one and one half *ri* perfectly naked, with a pistol in one hand and my sword in the other. It was still dark and I had to be very careful not to go in the wrong direction. I ran and ran, almost breathless, along the river bank. On my way back I happened to hear the voice of Paymaster Mishima, who was directing the conveyance of provisions. Still running, I shouted to him: "Paymaster Mishima! Provisions are of no use. We march again at once." When I had finished the sentence Mishima's voice was heard far behind me. Fortunately I did not lose myself nor make any mistake and reached our bivouac at ten minutes before five. The assembly was sounded at once and the order to attack was given. The orderly to whom I intrusted my clothing had not yet returned. In the early morning of a summer day it was nice and cool

第二十

without anything on, but I could not well march in that state. My last duty was done satisfactorily without uniform, but the next one seemed to require it. Another orderly was dispatched in search of the first one, but still the latter was not forthcoming. The time had come for us to start. I was in a very awkward plight, when at the last moment my uniform bearer came, and I was saved the distinction of a naked fight. It is a mere joke now, but I was exceedingly anxious then.

In this way the most delightful attack and advance was begun just as had been previously planned. We saw that it was to be a regular open field battle. That is to say, the skirmishers forming the first line advanced steadily, followed by the reserve body; all was arranged like a field manœuvre in time of peace. Such a movement is almost impossible in an attack on a fortress, which requires a gradual increase of reserves according to the circumstances of every hour and the condition of the ground at each point. Hitherto we had been attacking only rocky, hilly places, so that the only thing we could do was to be as near the enemy as possible, in order to seize the right opportunity to fall upon his forces with one accord. In this mode of attack we could not of course keep to the regular formation of a drill book. However, when once our army went past Taipo-shan, from there as far as the towering Taku-shan the ground was an extensive rolling country; hence the possi-

bility of our first open field battle. Our delight was
immense. Moreover, we took full advantage of the
lack of preparation of our opponent and made a
sudden attack. Although the Russians offered some
obstinate resistance, they were obliged to retire step
by step. Our regiment held only two companies
in reserve; all the rest were on the line of fire, and
gradually surrounded the enemy, engaging them on
both wings, with the result that when their centre
was defeated they were cut in two and forced to retreat.

Before reaching our final position, I was running
over a millet field carrying the regimental colors,
when I came across Major Achino. His sharp eyes
were sparkling like a hawk's, and he was standing
on a rock leaning on his sword. He and I had been
together at the headquarters of our regiment at
home, and I was one of those who was most influ-
enced by his character. His clear views on tactics,
his spirit of indomitable courage, his frank but dig-
nified demeanor, compelled my admiration. This
was the man who wrote that letter of farewell to our
colonel in the midst of our attack on Taipo-shan,
who rushed up the northeast corner of the hill with
two companies of his choicest men under him, and
thus opened the way for the other divisions to attack the enemy. I had not seen this gallant warrior since that time, and when I met him in the millet
field, I felt as if I actually saw him fighting in that

第二十

brave manner and could not repress my feeling of admiration and respect. I called out, "Major Achino!" and he gave me a glance and a word of encouragement, saying, "Add to the glory of your colors." I involuntarily bowed my head in recognition and gratitude, but we had no time for further conversation. We soon lost sight of each other, I marching forward and thinking fondly of him.

At this moment the enemy were gradually falling back before us; eventually they forsook their last line of resistance near Lung-tu and retreated toward Taku-shan. Now was the time for a prolonged pursuit. It is a delightful business to pursue a flying enemy, when they are shot from behind and fall like leaves in the autumnal wind. Such an opportunity generally comes after a fierce hard struggle, but on this particular occasion we had only about thirty casualties during the day. Such a pleasant chase after such an easy battle was something we might never expect to have again.

At noon of this day our army was in complete possession of the position we had had in view, and our line extended from the heights of T'uchêng-tsu in the north to the eastern heights of Taku-shan in the south. Standing on this newly acquired line with field-glass in hand, what a prospect greeted our eyes!

Here for the first time we could see the main defense line of the impregnable fortress of Port Arthur. Beginning with Kikuan-shan in the south, as far north as the eye could reach forts and trenches were visible all over the country. From among them some horrible-looking things were thrusting up their heads like tigers and leopards ready to spring; these were the heavy guns. Here, there, and everywhere, eight- to ten-fold wires were clustered together, dimly visible through the mist; these were wire-entanglements. The enemy's sentinels, or "far-looking scouts," could also be seen at different points. Men in groups of twenty or thirty were setting up wire-entanglements. This was the stage where we were to decide the points at issue, the stage on which the eyes of the world were fixed and which we actors could not forget even in sleep. Those who died prematurely, crying, "Port Arthur" or "Revenge," how boundless their joy would have been if they had survived to see this heart-stirring prospect! From this day on we were stationed in the vicinity of Lung-tu and began to construct strong works along the heights of Kanta-shan, with a view to first storming and taking Taku-shan and Hsiaoku-shan in front of the enemy's right wing, and then with these two hills as our base of attack to beginning an assault on their main line of defense.

I must say here with great respect that the Field-Marshal Commander-in-chief sent us the following Imperial message with regard to the battle of the 26th–30th of July, which even his humblest servant, like myself, had the honor of perusing: "The investing army having repeatedly braved the natural advantages of the advance positions of the fortress of Port Arthur, and having fought an arduous fight for several days, and having at last driven the enemy within their main line of defense, we are deeply gratified with your valor."

The commander sent His Majesty the following reply: "Your Majesty has graciously given us a special message in regard to our victory in the battle preparatory to the attack on the fortress of Port Arthur, and we are deeply affected. We Your Majesty's servants expect to exert ourselves still more zealously and accomplish the object of our army without failure. Respectfully submitted."

H. I. M. the Empress also sent us the following message: "Her Majesty the Empress has heard that the investing army has braved the dangers of Port Arthur Fortress and that an arduous attack has been successful after some days' continuance, and Her Majesty is deeply struck with the loyalty and valor of the officers and men of the army."

Our commander made reply also to this gracious message.

Since we, then, humble subjects without any special merit were thus recognized and encouraged by Their Majesties, how could we set at ease Their Majesties' revered hearts? It is hard to return even one thousandth part of their favor; a hot fight of a few days is nothing for us. These Imperial messages simply put us to shame and caused us to fear lest we might fail to deserve Their Majesties' boundless love and indulgence. The spirits of those loyal and brave ones who died in battle must have shed tears of gratitude on hearing these gracious messages.

After the Imperial messages came all were stirred, and the morale of the whole army became still more satisfactory. Steep hills and strong forts before us, and the gallant enemy defending them, must all yield to faithful subjects who are so anxious to set at ease Their Majesties' troubled hearts!

第二十一

THE STORMING OF TAKU–SHAN

UPON the seacoast east of the great fortress there is a rugged mountain towering high with almost perpendicular sides, its beetling rocks and crags spotted here and there with dwarf trees. The whole looks, from a distance, like an old tiger squatting on a hill. This is Taku-shan, or the Great Orphan. Hsiaoku-shan, or the Little Orphan, lies to the south, and on the opposite side, at the foot of Laolütszu. Taku-shan is a solitary peak 188 metres in height; its southwestern side looks down into the fortress of Port Arthur, and its northwestern side overlooked the inside of the line of investment formed by our left and central columns. Our works of investment, the movements of every division, and the position of our artillery were plainly visible from there. The side facing our army was particularly steep and precipitous, almost impossible to climb. It was as bad as Kenzan and Taipo-shan. While these two hills allowed the enemy to look into our position, they could not help becoming the mark and target for our fire. The commanding general of

174

our division made the following remark about them: —

"The Great and Little Orphans may be likened to the meat between the ribs of a chicken, which is hard to get and yet we are reluctant to throw it away.[1] As long as these hills are left in the enemy's hands, we are sure to be overlooked and shot from them, even though after we have taken them ourselves we cannot help becoming a target for the enemy."

Such a naturally protected position is extremely hard to take, and harder to keep, even when we have succeeded in taking it after untold struggles, because it will be fired at by all the neighboring forts as a convenient object. Therefore, in spite of the unanimous conclusion of the staff that the place must be taken from geographic and strategic necessity, we waited for the proper opportunity without firing a shot, though the enemy fired at us incessantly; and we hurried on our preparations for the close investment.

The 7th of August was finally fixed for our march and attack. Our field-artillery and siege-artillery, with shrapnels and mortars, had already taken their position in great secrecy. At 4 P. M. all the guns simultaneously opened fire, and directed it to the sky-line of both Orphans.

The boom and roar rent the air and white smoke

[1] A Chinese expression.

shut out the sky, and not only the forts on both Orphans, but also those on Panlung, Kikuan-shan, and Laolütszu in the rear responded to our fire at once. As far as the eye could reach the whole country was covered with smoke, and the tremendous noise of a hundred thunders at the same time went ceaselessly through the gloomy sky, which threatened rain at any moment. Whenever one of our shells struck a rock on Taku-shan, light yellowish-white sparks and fragments of rock flew far and wide — truly it was one of the sublimest sights of war. The enemy's artillery was superior in strength and they had the great advantage of overlooking us, hence our artillery labored under great difficulty and disadvantage and suffered damage of great magnitude. But the enemy's artillery seemed ignorant of the fact that our shrapnel guns and mortars were posted in the valley; they merely concentrated their fire on the artillery belonging to the columns, and on our infantry. Thus our big guns remained entirely free from damage, and toward sunset their effect on the enemy became more apparent, so that the Russian guns on Taku-shan seemed more or less silenced. At 4 P. M. our regiment left its place of bivouac and began to march, with a view to crossing the river Taiko and attacking the enemy as soon as our guns should open a proper opportunity for such an assault.

Before proceeding to describe this fierce struggle,

176

let me tell you what I had thought and done just before it. This experience was not mine only, but rather common to all fighters before a decisive battle. You will understand by this story one of the weaknesses of soldiers. During the three months since I had first stepped on the soil of Liaotung, I, humble and insignificant as I was, had borne the grave responsibility of carrying the regimental colors representing the person of His Majesty himself, and had already gone through three battles — on Kenzan, Taipo-shan, and Kanta-shan. Fortunately or unfortunately, I had not had a scratch as yet, while a large number of brave men had fallen under the standard, and the standard itself had been torn by the enemy's shell. When the regimental flag was damaged, a soldier quite close by me was killed and yet I remained unhurt. However, the rumors of my death had repeatedly reached home by this time, and a false story of my being wounded had appeared in the newspapers. I had heard of all this while at the front. One of these rumors said that at the time of our landing the storm was so violent that my sampan was upset and I was swallowed by big waves, and that, though I swam for several *cho*[1] with the regimental flag in my mouth, I was at last buried in the sea by the angry billows. Another rumor reported that I had encountered the enemy soon after landing and was killed, together with the captain of

[1] One *cho* equals .07 of a mile.

our First Company. All these mistaken reports had already made me a hero, and later I was frequently reported to have been wounded, with wonderful details accompanying each story. But when I examined myself I felt that I had no merit, neither the slightest wound upon my body. I could not help being ashamed of myself, and thought I was unworthy the great expectations of my friends. This idea made me miserable. So therefore I made up my mind to fight desperately and sacrifice my life at this battle of Taku-shan. A few days before the attack began, I told my servant that I was fully determined to die this time; that I did not know how to thank him for all his great goodness to me, and asked him to consider the assurance of my death as my only memento of my gratitude to him — I also asked him to fight valiantly. My servant, his eyes dim with tears, said that if his lieutenant died he would die with him. I told him that I would prepare a box for my ashes, but that, if I should be so beautifully killed as to leave no bones, he was to send home some of my hair. Then I went on to make a box of fragments of planks that had been used for packing big shells; they were fastened together with bamboo nails made by my servant. A clumsy box of about three inches square was thus prepared, in which I placed a lock of my hair, as well as sheets of paper for wrapping up my ashes; on the lid of the box I wrote my name and my posthumous Buddhistic

178

name as well. My coffin being thus ready, the only
thing remaining for me to do was to exert myself
to the very last, to repay the favor of the Emperor
and of the country with my own life. But, after all,
this box has not borne the distinction of carrying
my remains. Alas! it is now a mere laughing-stock
for myself and my friends.

That evening I wrote a letter to my elder brother
in Tokyo and reported to him the recent events in
the struggle, and told him that our attack was to
begin on the morrow; that I was ready and determined to die; that though my body be lost at Port
Arthur, my spirit would not forget loyalty to the
Emperor for seven lives. Of course this was meant
as my eternal farewell. On the same day I received
a letter from that brother, in which I found the following passages of admonition: —

"Think not of honor or of merit — only be faithful to thy duty."

"When Nelson died a glorious death in the sea-
fight of Trafalgar, he said, 'Thank God, I have
done my duty.'"

On the eve of this great battle I received these
words of encouragement and instruction, which
made my heart still braver and my determination
still firmer.

At 5 P. M. on the 7th of August, a great downpour of rain mingled with the thunder of cannon,
and the afternoon sky became utterly dark, dismal,

肉
弾

and dreary. We were halted on an eminence over the river Taiko, waiting anxiously for the command "Forward!" The rain became heavier and the sky darker. The Russian search-light, falling on one side of the hills and valleys, occasionally threw a whitish-blue light over the scene and impeded the march of our infantry. The plunging fire of the enemy became more and more violent as time went on. It made a strange noise, mingled with the tremendous downpour of rain. Lieutenant Hayashi and myself under one overcoat would exchange words now and then.

"We may separate at any moment," was Hayashi's abrupt remark, as if he were thinking of his death.

"I also am determined to die to-night," was my response. Whereupon Hayashi said:—

"What a long time we have been together!"

We had no more chance to continue this conversation, but had to separate. We had been comrades through the campaign, and while at home had been messmates for a long time. It was this Lieutenant Hayashi who, at the last rush upon Taipo-shan, achieved the first entry within the enemy's ramparts brandishing his sword. This hurried farewell was indeed our last — our hand-shaking an eternal good-by.

As was said before, our artillery fire began to take effect toward evening. Whereupon our detachment

began to advance as had been previously planned.
The rain fell more and more heavily, and the narrow paths became mud-holes. We marched with
great difficulty knee-deep in water and mud. The
enemy's battery on Taku-shan was not silenced or
weakened as we had supposed. As soon as they discovered us marching through the rain and smoke,
they resumed their firing with fresh vigor. When
we reached the river, the muddy water was over-
running its banks, and we did not know how deep
it was. The enemy, taking advantage of the heavy
rain, had dammed the stream below, and was trying
to impede our march by this inundation. However
brave we might be, we could not help hesitating before this unexpected ally of the Russians. Should
we brave the water, we might merely drown, instead of dying by the enemy's projectiles. But behold! a forlorn hope of our engineers jumped into
the dark flood and broke the dam; very soon the
water subsided and the infantry could cross the
river. Our whole force jumped into the water and
waded. Instead of being drowned, many were
killed in the stream by the enemy's fire; their
dead bodies were strewn so thick that they formed
almost a bridge across the river.

At last we reached the foot of Taku-shan, but
we had then to break the wire-entanglements and
run the risk of stepping on mines. One danger over,
others were awaiting us! This was not, however,

肉
彈
the time or place to hesitate; we began to clamber over rocks and scale precipices. Pitch darkness and violent rain increased our difficulties. The pouring rain and the crossing of the river had wet us through and through, yet we could not exercise our muscles freely to promote the circulation of blood. Moreover, as we came nearer and nearer the Russian trenches, they poured shrapnel bullets upon our heads, or hurled stones and beams upon us, so that the difficulty of pushing forward was very great. A neighboring detachment had already approached the skirmish-trenches which formed a horseshoe half-way up on the side of the mountain. Meanwhile our detachment was busy making firm footholds in the rocks on the mountain-side, preparing for an early opportunity of trying a night assault. But the enemy with search-light and star-shells worked so hard to impede progress, that the night surprise was given up as an impossibility. Accordingly we planned an attack at early dawn instead; we had now to wait, facing each other and the enemy, exposed to the rain, which continued to fall without intermission.

When the eastern sky began to lighten, the rain was still falling. The bodies of our comrades scattered along the river Taiko could not be picked up, nor could an orderly reach the other side of the stream, because we were right under the enemy's eyes. In spite of this, orderlies were dispatched, but were shot down without a single exception. Such a horrible scene! Such a disappointing result! No one had any plan to propose, and we did not know when and how the object of storming the enemy could be accomplished. Sergeant-Major Iino, who was shot through the abdomen and lying flat in agony at the foot of Taku-shan, was at this moment begging every orderly that passed by to kill him and relieve his suffering. How could we defeat the enemy and care for the dead and wounded? Our minds ran right and left, but still no desirable opportunity offered itself. On the top of all this, eleven ships of the Russian fleet, including the Novic, made their appearance near Yenchang and began bombarding our infantry marching toward the Taku and Hsiaoku-shan from the rear. There was nothing to shield us; we became a certain target for the enemy's fire, and were killed and wounded at their will. We were thus reduced to a state of uttermost desperation, as if a wolf had attacked us at the back gate while we were defending the front gate against a tiger. But, after all, how did we capture this Taiku-shan?

第二十二

SUN FLAG ON TAKU-SHAN

THE powder-smoke covering the whole scene was like surging waves, and the dark shower of rain may be likened to angry lions. Above us the steep mountain stood high, kissing the heavens — even monkeys could hardly climb it. Each step upward presented a still steeper place — one precipice climbed brought us to another still harder. And the fierce Russian eagle threatened us from the top of this formidable height. All our fire from every direction was being concentrated upon the enemy's position on Taku-shan. To respond to this attack, the Russian big guns were putting out red tongues at us in front, and from behind their war-ships were coming to shatter our backs. The enemy, with this natural advantage and with this strong defensive array, was not easy to defeat. But if we failed to take this place, not only would our whole army be checked here and be unable to assault the great fortress, but also we should be without any base for investing Port Arthur. Hence the urgent necessity

184

of storming the enemy irrespective of any amount of sacrifice and difficulty.

Our regiment spent that night and morning on the hillside, exposed to heavy rain and strong fire. But at about 3 P. M. the right opportunity for us to attack the enemy offered itself. Our siege-gunners had so successfully bombarded the enemy's ships that they were obliged to retreat for a while, and gave us more freedom of action. When this opportunity came, the brigadier-general gave us the following order: "The left wing is now to storm Taku-shan, and your regiment, in connection with the left wing, is to attack the northern slope."

At the same time we received the following intimation from the commander of the left wing: "Our regiment is now starting for an assault irrespective of damage — I hope that your regiment also will join in this memorable assault and occupy Taku-shan with us."

As soon as this order was made public, both wings started at the same time. All of us braved the anger and fury of the king of hell, braved the natural steepness and formidable fire, and attacked and pressed upward with strength and courage as of the gods. The shriek and yell of men, the boom and roar of guns, the gleam of bayonets and swords, the flying of dust, the flowing of blood, the smashing of brains and bowels — a grand confusion and a tremendous hand-to-hand fight! The enemy rolled

185

肉
彈
down huge stones from the top, and many an unfortunate was thrown into the deep valley or crushed against the rocks. Shrieks of pain and yells of anger made the whole scene more like hell than like this world. The heavy batteries of Kikuan-shan and Erhlung-shan were well aimed and their shells exploded right over the top of Taku-shan, while fiery bundles of spherical shells and fougasse presented long lines of bright light crossing and intersecting from all directions. Presently a great shout of Banzai shook the whole mountain, rising from top and foot simultaneously. What? What had happened? Behold, a flag is waving in the dark clouds of smoke! Is it not our dear Rising Sun? Our assault has succeeded! Our standard is already unfurled on the top of the hill! We saw this and we cried for joy.

Taku-shan, enshrouded in its light gray dress of smoke, was now ours. But as soon as it came into our possession, all the fortresses of the enemy began concentrating their fire upon our main position on this mountain. Heavy-gun shells, as big as a common water jar,[1] came whizzing like locomotives, causing heavy vibrations in the air. When they exploded with a tremendous noise, a miraculous light glittered where the white smoke rose, and rocks were shattered where the dark cloud hung. It

[1] The large earthenware jar, or reservoir, used for holding the water supply of a Japanese kitchen. They vary in size, but the smallest will hold several gallons.

186

seemed as if the very centre of the earth were shaken, and the bodies of the dead were cut into small fragments. Our position was far from safe. Our detachments occupying the new place could hardly keep their post. If the enemy should try a counter-assault, as they were sure to, how could we keep them in check on such a perilous mountain-top? If we even stretched our necks to look across the slopes into the enemy's defenses, we were sure to be visited by their fire at once. We could not move a step. One soldier, who was on guard over six field-guns captured on the top, was hit by a whole shell and literally shattered to bits. One piece of his flesh, which flew above our heads and stuck to a rock behind us, was all that was left of him. Another shell fell into a group of soldiers, and twenty-six men became small dust in one minute; the rock that was shattered by this shell buried alive three more.

Lieutenant Kunio Segawa was shot through the abdomen on this day; toward evening his end seemed near. His servant and others were nursing him, when his elder brother, Captain Segawa, who knew nothing of his wound, happened to come along and was asked to give his dying brother the farewell drink of water. Whereupon the captain quickly came near to his brother and shouted, "Kunio!" As soon as the dying man heard his dear brother's voice, as if he had been thinking

肉
弾

of him and longing to see him, he opened his dim eyes in the midst of his hard breathing, gazed on his brother's face, grasped his hand firmly with tears, and for a while both were silent with emotion. The captain said presently: "Kunio, you have done well! Have you anything to say?" and he wiped his dying brother's face and poured water into his mouth from his water bottle. The younger brother faintly nodded and said, "Dear elder brother!" [1]

That was his last word, and soon he started for another world. What was the grief of the surviving brother then! The bystanders could not repress tears of sympathy for both. Two weeks later, in the battle of August 24, the captain followed his beloved brother and joined the ranks of those who were not.

Taku-shan, the keystone to their main line of defense, being now wrested from their hands, the Russians must have been very indignant and greatly disappointed. As was expected, they tried counter-attacks over and over again with a view to retaking Taku-shan, but each time we repulsed them and reduced them to deeper disappointment. A

[1] The distinction between elder and younger brother is so great in the Japanese mind that there is no common word for the relationships, but *ani*, elder brother, and *ototo*, younger brother, are as distinct as brother and sister with us. *Ani* in address is softened to "Nii San."

few days after the occupation of Taku-shan, one
of the sentinels stationed at the top of the mountain
was unexpectedly shot and killed at early dawn by
a Russian scout. Ready to encounter the enemy, the
Second Company ran up to the top, where they saw,
only ten or fifteen feet below them, some Russian
officers at the head of over seventy men brandishing their swords and hurrying up the mountain.
Without a moment's hesitation, a fierce rifle fire
was directed at the enemy, who seemed startled
by this unexpected reception and, turning, took to
their heels and ran away, almost rolling and tumbling in their haste. Our company took this good
opportunity and shot them right away. What a
splendid result! Not one of them was left alive!
Their bodies made dark spots scattered over the
mountain-side. At that very moment a large detachment of the enemy was stationed as a reinforcement at the point where the roads branch toward
Hsaioku-shan and toward our position on Taku-
shan. Their plan was probably this: an advance
detachment was sent to both mountains, and this
reinforcing body was to hurry to whichever hill
should offer the better opportunity for a counter-
attack. Such a half-hearted, uncertain policy can
never succeed.

However, as has been repeatedly remarked, the
stubborn pertinacity of the Russians was something
that surprised us. When any position is attacked,

肉
彈

the loss of one part of it may necessitate the retreat of its defenders in another part, with the alternatives of annihilation or of being made captives: in such a case, the Russian soldiers will not vacate the spot, but stick firmly to it until they are killed. Even when they are reduced to one single man, that one man will still continue shooting; if we go near him, he will fix his bayonet and fight on obstinately until finally an idea of surrender suggests itself to his mind. Such things happened frequently at Kenzan, at Taipo-shan, and at Taku-shan. I am told that after the battle of Nanshan, mysterious shot came flying, whence no one knew, and killed or wounded more than ten of our men. After long search it was found that a Russian soldier was hiding himself in a kitchen and shooting us from the window eagerly and fearlessly. Whenever we asked Russian captives why they resisted us so stubbornly, they were sure to answer: "We could not disobey the officer's command." We had heard of the absolute, obsequious obedience of the Russian soldiers, and here on the real battle-field we found that it was true and that they were faithful to their duty unto death. This perhaps comes from the fact that the old relation between the nobility and serfs in the Middle Ages is now kept up between Russian officers and men. This Russian spirit of obedience is totally different in origin from the unfeigned harmony and friendliness and the sincere, voluntary obedience obtaining through all the ranks of the Japanese Army. An English officer, who spent several months in Manchuria with the Japanese Army, remarked that the strongest characteristic and the most attractive thing about it was the friendly harmony prevailing from the top to the bottom, the like of which could not be found in the army of any other nation, not even in England or in democratic America. Perhaps the real strength of our army comes from this special moral and spiritual condition. But the obstinate courage of the Russian soldiers is a characteristic worthy of our admiration. While holding fast to Port Arthur, their provisions and ammunition became scarce, thousands and tens of thousands of lives were taken, and their sad situation was like a light before a gust of wind; yet, in the midst of such disheartening conditions, they did not change their attitude at all, but went on resisting us with dogged determination. This was done by the Russians through the force of their Russian characteristics and shows plainly what was the education and discipline they had undergone. A passage in the Military Reader of Russia runs: —

"The laurel of victory in battle can be won by the bayonet and the war-cry. When your shot is exhausted, knock down the enemy with the stock of your rifle. If the rifle stock be broken, bite with your teeth."

Yes, they were stubborn in their resistance and attack, but at the same time they were extremely careful of their lives. These two characteristics are contradictory to each other. "Rather live as a tile than be broken as a jewel," seemed their great principle, the contrary of the Japanese ideal, "rather die beautifully than live in ignominy." One Russian captive is reported to have said: "I have a dear wife; she must be extremely anxious about me. Our officers told us that the Japanese Army was brittle as a clay statue. But, contrary to our expectation, they are as strong as devils. Rather than fight and be killed, I must save my life for my wife. If I die she will grieve and go mad. I am no match for the Japanese. It is silly to fight on, knowing that we shall surely be killed by the Japanese Army." There is an impassable gulf between this and the Japanese ideal and determination to die in honor but never live in shame.

We defended and held on to this Taku-shan, though it was extremely difficult to hold against the enemy's assault. Fortunately all their attempts at retaking it came to naught. Eventually the Russians seemed to give up the idea of any further counter-attack, and began to busy themselves with strengthening the already strong constructions on the main line of defense and with impeding our work of fortification by firing incessantly the heavy guns of the different forts. At the same time, our detachment was fortifying Taku-shan on the side toward the enemy, gathering siege material, constructing strong positions for heavy batteries, and sending out efficient scouts to ascertain the positions of the enemy's mines, the condition of their wire-entanglements, and to see how their fire would affect the routes assigned for our march. All these preparations, and all these investigations about the condition of the zone of our attack being completed, the 19th of August was fixed for the first general assault, and East Kikuan was given to our detachment as our chief objective. Because this battle was expected to seal the fate of Port Arthur, everything was most carefully and accurately planned and mapped out.

第二十三

PROMOTION AND FAREWELLS

OF course we left Japan fully determined to
turn into dust under the hoofs of His Majesty's steed, saying, "Here I stand ready to die."
Our hearts were impatient, but the opportunity
was slow in coming. More than one hundred
days had passed since we had left for the front.
Then hundreds of blossoms on home fields and
mountains made our uniforms fragrant with their
sweet smell, the spring breeze that wafted us to a
strange land far away lightly kissed the sun-colors.
Time flies quickly, and now we sit under the shadow
of green leaves. At night, sleeping on our arms, or
in the day, exposed to the hail-storm of bullets, we
had never forgotten our desire to return the Imperial
favor and beneficence with death, and death only.
The time, however, was not yet full. Thousands
of our comrades had died without the joy of seeing
the final success; their spirits must be unconsoled
and unable to find eternal rest. We were eager to
avenge them, but ah! the opportunity had not yet

194

come. We survivors lived in the stink of rotting flesh and crumbling bones; our own flesh wasted and even our bones seemed thinner. We were like a group of spirits with sharp, eager passions in miserable bodies, but still we were offshoots of the genuine cherry tree of Yamato. How was it that we were still alive after fighting one, two, three, already four battles, without having fallen like beautiful cherry petals of the battle-field? I had been fully resolved to die on Taku-shan, but still I was left behind by a great many of my friends. Surely this time, in this general assault, I must have the honor and distinction of offering my little self to our beloved country. With this idea, this desire, this determination, I started for the battle.

I was promoted to first lieutenant in the early part of August, but the news reached me just on this occasion. Colonel Aoki called me before him and told me most gravely: "I congratulate you on your promotion. You have carried the regimental colors from the very beginning. You are now released from that duty, but strive harder still, for to-morrow is assigned for our general assault. I have eaten and slept with you for a long time and am grieved to part with you, but I say good-by to you now because I am anxious for your success."

Yes, I had eaten and slept with the dear regimental commander from our first arrival and had fought at his side. In the bivouac, exposed to rain and dew, the colonel had shared his mat with me so that I might sleep the better. Even his scanty food he divided with me, smiling as cheerily as if he were eating with his family at home. I had always feared that the colonel, who was used to sleeping on a comfortable couch at home, might contract an illness from this bed and pillow of grass. With three thousand lives in his hand, the life of the regimental commander is very precious, and the morale of the whole regiment depends largely upon his health. I had tried my best to serve him attentively and make him as comfortable as the uncomfortable circumstances of the battle-field would allow. Some time ago, while we were at Changchia-tun, I prepared hot water in a water jar and offered him the first hot bath he had had since leaving Japan. He was pleased with it from the bottom of his heart, and I shall never forget his glad countenance of that moment. Now I had to part with the colonel who was as dear to me as my own father, and my grief was without limit. Of course I still belonged to one of his companies and I was still his subordinate. It was not a real separation, but I felt as if I were going far away from him. When I heard these farewell words of his, I felt my throat choked with tears and could not raise my head for a while. It was also a great sorrow for me to part with the regimental colors

196

that I had taken care of through thick and thin.
When I looked at the faded, torn standard now
hanging to the left of the colonel, I could not help
feeling that among the three thousand men whose
hearts all stir at the sight of that flag, I had a
right to a special emotion in the presence of the
regimental insignia.

After a moment of thoughtful silence, I sorrowing over my separation from the flag and the colonel,
and the colonel apparently regretting his parting
with me, I said earnestly: "Colonel, I will show
you what a splendid fight I can make — " I could
not say anything more and, turning on my heel
quietly, walked off a few steps and then ran to
my servant and said: "I am now ordered to go to
my company. You, in consequence, must leave me,
but I shall never forget your kindness. Remember me as your true elder brother to eternity. I
cannot say anything more. Fight like a brave
soldier."

Bunkichi Takao, my servant soldier, wept bitterly and said he could never leave me. That, however, could not be. I soothed and comforted him,
saying that he must obey his superiors' commands
faithfully and not be behind anybody else in doing
and suffering, and that the box we had made together before the battle of Taku-shan was certainly
to be used this time. I, too, was very reluctant to
lose him, and my heart was full of emotion.

肉
弾

"Lieutenant, do you really think of me as your younger brother?" Takao said, in tears; and I too shed hot tears.

"We part now, but may meet again. If we die, let us die together a glorious death and talk over the past together in another world." So saying, I started to go after he had brushed the dust off my uniform and retied the strings of my leggings.

"Well, then, lieutenant — " he began to say, but, too sad to look at me any longer, he covered his face and turned away.

"Takao, don't forget what I have told you from time to time," I said, and walked to the position where the Third Battalion was stationed.

Separated from the regimental flag, from the colonel, and from my own servant, I directed my solitary steps through the wild country. As I looked at the hills and valleys, now turned into the graves of my dear comrades, and watched the clouds gather and disperse in the sky, I could not help thinking of the inconstancy of earthly things. Suddenly it occurred to me that I must see Surgeon Yasui once more, and say good-by to Captain Matsuoka, my senior officer from my native province. At once I turned back and walked some distance to a ravine at the northern foot of Taku-shan. Captain Matsuoka was sitting alone in his tent and was glad to see me.

"I have not seen you for some time," he said. "Are you quite well?"

"Thank you, I am, and I have been promoted to be first lieutenant. I am now ordered to join the Third Battalion. Please continue your favor toward me."

The captain said, abruptly, "Then this is our last chance of meeting in this world!"

I told him that I, too, expected to die, and expressed my desire that we might die together on the top of Kikuan. When I rose to go, the captain tapped me on the shoulder and asked, "What have you there at your belt?" Whereupon I smiled faintly and said, "It is my coffin." "Well, indeed! You are well prepared!" That was our farewell, and I left the ravine. Soon this separation in life was to be followed by the separation of death.

I then went over to the headquarters of the First Battalion, which were hidden behind the rocks near Chuchia-tun, and found Surgeon Yasui. Soon after my arrival there, a few of the enemy's shot fell with a tremendous noise in front of the tent. Four or five more followed, but we were so accustomed to such things that we paid little attention to it. This position, I was told, was frequently a target for the enemy's fire. I was grieved to hear that the commander of the First Battalion had been slightly wounded in the battle of Taku-shan. When I told Surgeon Yasui of my promotion, he took me aside to where the powder-boxes were piled and said that he had been longing to see me; that, though we

第二十三

肉
彈

were in the same place, we had had no chance of a friendly chat, and that every day and night he had been waiting impatiently to hear from me. I was deeply moved and said to him that it was strange that both of us had been spared so far, but that this time I was fully prepared for death, and that I had come on purpose to see him once more and take a last farewell. I also reminded him of our promise in that ruined house at Hwangni-chuan, and said that if both should die that would be all, but if he should survive me he was to cut off a part of my bloodstained uniform and keep it as a memento. We grasped each other's hands firmly, saying that this was our eternal farewell in this world, and, praying for each other's success, we parted in tears. Reluctantly I left his tent, crossed the river Taiko, climbed the mountain slope facing the enemy's fortress, and went to the headquarters of the brigade to pay my respects to the brigadier-general. Just at the time when I arrived at head-quarters the adjutant was relieved from duty on account of illness, so, as a temporary arrangement, I was put in his place as aide-de-camp. Later I was put in charge of the Twelfth Company.

On the night previous to the beginning of the general attack of the 19th, I received two letters brought to me by the cook. Of course no mail was expected to reach us in such a place and under such circumstances, but these two letters

had been miscarried and mislaid for some time before finally reaching me. They were both from my
elder brother, one inclosing a fountain pen and
the other a photograph of my two little nieces, one
four and the other three years of age. They seemed
to say "Dear Uncle" to me from the picture. Such
sweet little faces! If, however, the little babies in
the photograph had had eyes that could see, they
would perhaps have cried at my changed, emaciated features. Night and day I had been seeing
nothing but unkempt soldiers or shattered flesh
and broken bones. Even the flowers that had
smiled from the grassy fields were now trodden
down and crushed. In such a battle-field, and on
the night before a great fight, I was honored with
the visit of these dear nieces. How it softened my
wild heart! What joy they brought to me! I could
not help kissing their dear eyes and mouths and
murmuring to myself: "You brave little ones, that
have left your dear mother's lap to cross the broad
sea and wild waves to visit me in this place of
powder-smoke and shot-rain! Your uncle will take
you with him to-morrow and let you see how he
chastises the enemy of dear Japan."

The cloud of smoke had passed away for this
night and bright stars were twinkling in the sky.
I slept in the camp with my two little nieces by
my side. Nelson's last words came forcibly to my
mind, and I also repeated over and over again the

肉
彈
couplet that I had written and given my father when leaving Japan, in which I had spoken of "the glory of death in battle, loyalty for seven lives." To leave my skull bleaching in the wilderness and become a patriotic spirit returning to life seven times — was this to take place on the morrow or on the day after? My time was almost full!

There was a lance-corporal by the name of Yamamoto, who about this time sent clippings of his nails and hair to his mother and brother, together with a farewell letter and poem; and this letter proved to be his last. It ran thus: —

"Twice already I have joined a forlorn hope, and still I am keeping my head on my shoulders. I am filled with grief when I think of my dead comrades. Out of over two hundred men who advanced before the others of our company, there are only twenty left who are able-bodied. Fortunately or unfortunately I am among this small number. But the life of man is only fifty years. Unless I give up that life betimes, I may have no proper opportunity again. Sooner or later I must die, as all must die. So I prefer being broken to pieces as a jewel to remaining whole as a tile. Shot or bayonet or whatever may come, I can die but once. My comrade is shot at my right hand, my officer's thigh and arm are blown up into the air at my left — and I in the middle am not hurt at all, and

I pinch myself, doubting whether it is not a dream. I feel the pinching, so I must be alive still. My time for dying has not come yet. I must brace myself up to avenge my comrades. You proud, impudent Ruskies! I will chastise you severely. — Thus my heart is ever impatient though I am lacking in brilliant parts. Born a farmer's son, I shall yet be sung as a flower of the cherry tree, if I fight bravely and die in the battle-field, instead of dying naturally but ignobly in a thatched hut on a straw mat.

"Banzai, banzai, banzai to H. M. the Commander-in-chief!

"TAKETOSHI YAMAMOTO,

"Late Lance-Corporal of the Infantry of the Army."

You notice that he used the word "late" before his title, showing beyond any doubt his resolve to enter the death-ground with a smile. Such a resolve was held by all at that time, and Yamamoto only gave a clear though unsophisticated expression to the general sentiment.

第二十四

THE BEGINNING OF THE GENERAL ASSAULT

WHEN a correspondent of the "Novoe Vremya" inspected the defenses of Port Arthur, his remark is reported to have been: "It is like an eagle's nest that even a sky-scraping ladder cannot reach." Yes, it was even so. As far as the eye could reach, every hill and every mountain was covered with forts and ramparts; the landward side was encircled with iron walls of tenfold strength, and its defenders were brave soldiers trained by the veteran General Dragomiloff, — courageous men, the strongest and quickest, — the flower of the Russian Army. We were now in front of this "impregnable" fortress to prove that it was "pregnable" after all. The 19th of August was the first day of the general attack, the starting-point of the historic incident of the fall of Port Arthur. The struggle that was to be characterized in the world's history of warfare as the most difficult and most horrible of all struggles began on this day and lasted for more than four months. During this period our desperate attack was responded to by as desperate a defense, and our army paid an immense price for its victory, turning the mountains and valleys of Port Arthur into scorched earth honeycombed by shells, butchering men and capturing the fortress at last with bullets of human flesh shot out by the Yamato-Damashii itself. The gazing world was astonished by the wonderful efficiency of such a mode of warfare!

We, at the foot of Taku-shan, were hurrying on the various preparations for attack. We were making a special investigation of the ways and means of encountering the wire-entanglements, upon which the enemy depended as the most efficient of their secondary defensive works, and by the stakes and wires of which so many of our men had been killed in previous battles. All the hills in our sight, large or small, high or low, were wrapped about with these horrible things, that looked at a distance like dark dots on the ground.

We had to break these entanglements, step on them, and proceed. The cutting properly belonged to the engineers, but their number was limited while that of the wire-entanglements was almost limitless. So the infantry had to learn to cut them for themselves. An imitation entanglement was made on the bank of the river Taiko and we were taught by the engineers how to break it down.

First of all, a group of shears-men would march up and cut the iron wires, then the saw-men would follow and knock down the stakes or else saw them through. When a part of the entanglement was thus opened, a detachment of men would rush through the opening.

This kind of work was of urgent necessity for us and we practiced it with zeal and diligence. But in actual fighting the work cannot be done so easily. The forlorn-hope engineers, who march up to destroy the entanglements, are always annihilated without exception, because they have to work before the very muzzles of the machine-guns. Moreover, it was discovered that these wires were charged with electricity. There were, however, two opinions about the electric current: one was that the electricity was strong enough to kill whoever touched the wires, and the other that it was only intended to inform the enemy's watchtowers, by a weak current of electricity, of the approach of the destroyers. Whichever it might be, we could not cut the wires with ordinary scissors so long as they were charged with electricity, so we contrived to bind bamboo sticks to the handles of the shears to make them non-conducting. In spite of all these precautions, we found in actual fight that the wires were charged with a very strong current; some of our men were killed instantly by the shock, others had their limbs split like brushes of bamboo. We also practiced methods of crossing the enemy's trenches with ladders, but again in actual fight we found that their trenches were too wide or too deep for these ladders to be of much use.

The fortress was protected by earth-mines, which were buried everywhere. They had to be destroyed by our engineers, by cutting off the fuse. Until the very day of our attack we could see through field-glasses groups of Russians at work here and there, burying these explosives in the ground with picks. We marked those places on our maps. We found out and remembered everything that we could; for instance, that each of the stakes of the entanglements was beaten down with twelve blows of a hammer, or how many earth-mines were being buried in any particular valley. Our reconnoitring parties found that every ravine up which our infantry was likely to march was set with mines, and that the methods of disposing them were very clever. To cite one example, where the ravine was narrowest there was buried a mine that would explode when stepped on. When the first man was killed in this way, the rest would of course divide themselves on either side of the ravine, where a series of mines would burst and kill all of the attacking party. It was extremely hard to go through these places in safety. On the top of all this, all the guns and rifles of all the forts and skirmish-trenches were so directed as to be able to aim at every ravine

肉
弾

and every rock, so that none of us could escape the concentrated cross-fire from three directions. Their defense left almost nothing to be desired.

At dawn on the 19th of August, the whole line of our artillery opened fire simultaneously, with East Kikuan as our chief objective, but bombarding other forts at the same time. This was the first step in our general assault. Soon, our assaulting columns pushed on their way under cover of the artillery fire, approaching the enemy inch by inch, ready to rush upon them with one accord as soon as our fire began to take effect upon the Russians. Therefore our batteries devoted their whole energy to breaking the forts, shattering the bomb-proofs, and opening breaches in the skirmish-trenches through which our storming parties could enter.

No sooner had our firing begun than the enemy responded from all their batteries and tried hard to silence our artillery and impede the progress of our infantry. What a terrible scene presented itself when huge shells were exchanged between the heavy guns of both sides! Explosive shells as big as *saké*-casks [1] and spherical shells caused great vibrations in the air, and their groaning reverberation set at naught the fury of pealing thunders. The bursting of shells scattered lightning everywhere, and the smoke covered the scene with thick

[1] The *saké*-cask contains about sixteen gallons.

steamy clouds, in which it seemed impossible for
any living thing to breathe. We nicknamed the
enemy's shells "train shells," because they came
moaning and shrieking just like a train leaving the
station with sharp whistling. When we heard such
a sound near us the whole earth shook, and in the
tremendous roaring men, horses, rocks, and sand
were all hurled up together. Everything that came
into collision with these terrible trains was reduced
to small fragments; these fragments would fall to
the ground and then go up again, as if they had
wings to fly with. One lieutenant's neck was torn
by a fragment of shell, and his head hung by the
skin only. Both arms of a private were cut off clean
from the shoulders by the same process.

This day was to come to an end with bombardment only. It had been our plan to employ the first
day or two in bombarding the enemy and then
to go on with an infantry attack. That evening I
went on business to the headquarters of our division, that is, the place where our artillery was
posted. It was a dark night, and through the sky
whitish-blue bars of fire were flying to and fro between the contending parties; it looked to me like
the highway leading to hell. The Russian search-
lights were being thrown over the position of our
artillery from Kikuan-shan and Hokuginzan. These
terrible lights would turn every now and then toward our infantry, who were approaching the

enemy step by step. We, too, used the search-lights captured from the enemy and tried to counteract the power of theirs and also to expose the Russian battery to view, but they were far inferior to those still in the enemy's possession. Star-shells were shot off from time to time by the enemy, which illuminated the sky far better than the annual display of fireworks at Ryogoku.[1] They were like great electric lamps hanging in the air, making the whole place as light as day, so that even the movement of an ant could easily be detected. They were powerful in thwarting the progress of our assaulting column, because every movement of the detachment was exposed by this light and could be accurately seen by the enemy, and the usual machine-guns were sure to pour a rain of horrible shot upon the invaders. Therefore, as soon as we saw the star-rocket burst in the sky, we used to caution each other, saying, "Don't move! don't move!"

When I reached headquarters, the division-commander and his staff were standing at our artillery position and watching this scene of night fighting without the cover of darkness. As soon as a search-light was seen in a Russian fort, our chief-of-staff would order, "Hit that! Smash that fellow!" He said, folding his arms in utter unconcern: "I

[1] The annual festival of the "Opening of the River," held at Ryogoku Bashi in Tokyo, is the occasion for a great display of fireworks.

feel like a young bride! Exposed to such a full glare of light, I am awfully shy and bashful!"

Our detachment marched as far as Yangchia-kou during this night. Soon after we reached there, a shell came near us with a tremendous noise. We said to each other: "Some must have been killed. Who are they? Who?" When the smoke cleared, we found four or five men lying dead or wounded, two of them recruits who had arrived only a few days before from home. One of the two was killed in a horrible manner; the half of his body below the waist was entirely gone. The legs of the other were shattered and the blood was gushing out like water. His captain went to him and encouraged him, saying: "Don't be afraid! Be brave!"

"Captain, I am very sorry to be thus disabled without having fought at all. I will come back healed as quickly as possible. Please let me be in your company again."

"Even without having fought, your wounds are honorable. Get well quickly and come back!"

Why one is shot on the battle-field and the other not seems an inscrutable mystery. Some there are who in one severe fight after another do not sustain a single scratch; others seem to be followed by shot or to draw shot to themselves. Some are killed very soon after landing and before knowing how it feels to be shot at. When once you become a target for shot, forty or fifty may come to you, as

第二十四

to that man in the battle of Taipo-shan of whom I have already spoken. Is this what is called fate, or is it mere chance? On the 19th, when the headquarters of the division were removed to the northern slope of Taku-shan, the division-commander was observing the enemy, with a staff-officer on either side, when a projectile came and both the staff-officers were killed on the spot, while the general in the middle was not even slightly hurt. In an assault on a fortress those in front have of course the highest probability of being hit, but even those in the rear sustain more injury than in a field battle. Napoleon said: "A shot may be aimed at you, but cannot pursue you. If it could pursue you at all, it would overtake you even if you fled to the uttermost parts of the earth." Yes, a shot is an uncanny thing, like an apparition. With our human power we cannot tell whether it will hit us or not. It depends entirely upon one's luck. There is another incident that I recollect in this connection. After the battle of Taipo-shan, five or six of the retreating Russians were walking off in a leisurely way, without hurrying, and swinging their arms. This behavior we thought very impudent, and each of us aimed at them as carefully as in drill-ground practice and fired at them with our rifles resting on something steady, but all in vain. One officer was sure he could hit them, but he too failed, and the Russians continued to walk off slowly and were eventually lost sight of. Several times after this, we tried our skill in musketry on a Russian standing on a fort and waving his handkerchief to challenge us, or on some audacious fellow who would dare to come out of the breastwork and insult us. In spite of our skill, indignation, and curiosity combined, these impudent fellows often escaped in safety. Such being the case, those who have been through several battles become naturally careless and fearless. At first we involuntarily lower our heads a little at the sound of a small bullet. Even the officer who scolds his men, saying, "Who is it that salutes the enemy's shot?" cannot help nodding to the enemy at first. Of course this does not imply timidity at all; it seems to be the result of some sort of reflex action of the nerves. But when the shot begin to come like a shower of rain, we can no longer give each shot a bow, but become bold at once. The boom and roar of big shells excite in us no special sensation. When we know that by the time we hear these horrible sounds the projectiles have gone far past us, our courage is confirmed and, instead of bowing to an empty sound, we begin to think of standing on the breastwork and munching rice-balls to show off to the enemy! And the shot seems to shun those audacious ones as a rule, to go round them and call upon others!

第二十五

A RAIN OF HUMAN BULLETS

THE bodies of the brave dead built hill upon hill, their blood made streams in the valleys. The battle-field was turned into a cemetery and hill and valley into burnt-out soil. As minutes and seconds went on, life after life was sent off into eternity. When the attacking party combines accurate firearms with ammunition powerful enough to demoralize the enemy, what is the power with which to follow up this advantage to its sure result, that is, final victory? That power is the bayonet and the war-cry together! The glittering bayonet, the hideous yelling, when combined, are what really put the enemy to flight. A correspondent of the London "Standard" has said truly: "The war-cry of the Japanese Army pierced the hearts of the Russians." But, however much our glittering bayonets and shouting voices intimidated the enemy, I cannot help weeping at the recollection of that assault. Why? Because the glittering of the bayonet and the yelling of the war-cry became fainter and fainter in the first general assault! In spite of the great number of projectiles and the large quantity of human bullets that were spent, the storming of the forts which the Russians called invincible ended in utter failure. Nay, several great assaults after this one drained the blood of patriotic warriors and shattered their bones in vain. After all, however, this apparently useless sacrifice of a large number of lives was not without its effect. Strategically we needed to reduce the great fortress as quickly as possible, however great the damage to our army might be; so, therefore, the commanding general resolved with tears to offer the necessary sacrifice, and his subordinates willingly offered their lives and stormed the enemy with bullets of their own flesh. And these first fruitless assaults proved the necessary first step and a valuable preparation for our final success.

We noticed that our continuous bombardment of the Russian forts since the 19th, more especially of those on East Kikuan, which was our objective, had dealt a severe blow on the enemy; so the Yoshinaga battalion was ordered to march on the night of the 21st as the first assaulting column. A forlorn hope of engineers were dispatched ahead to break the wire-entanglements. Their desperate effort was fortunately successful, and a little opening was made for the infantry. Thereupon Captain Yoshinaga ordered his men

第二十五

肉
弾

not to fire a shot, not to utter a whisper, but to press on under cover of the night; and a body of dark shadows suddenly stood right against the enemy's ramparts. The surprised Russians were obliged to retreat without offering a fight; but as soon as they had fallen back a little distance, a large detachment of reinforcements appeared, accompanied by the horrible sound of machine-guns in the rear. They forced the retreating Russians forward, and together they offered a strong counter-attack, with their shout of "Woola" shaking heaven and earth. Major Yoshinaga ordered his men not to retreat a step, and a terrible hand-to-hand fight ensued. Both parties fought fiercely with fists, bayonets, and rifles, but alas! Major Yoshinaga, who was commanding his men from the breastwork, was shot through the chest and fell. Captain Okubo took up the command in his place; soon he too was killed. Substitute after substitute was killed, and eventually not only the officers but also the men were, nearly all of them, killed. No reinforcement came to their aid, the enemy's concentrated fire became more and more violent, and the few surviving men were obliged to retreat for a while into the ravine below the wire-entanglements and wait there for the arrival of reserves. None came to help them, and they waited vainly until the dusk of the following day, with the remains of their dead comrades before their eyes.

They were right below the enemy, only a dozen feet or so away from them, and for thirteen hours they had to grasp their rifles hard and stare at the Russians, unable to do anything.

On the night of the 22d the Taketomi battalion went through the broken wire-entanglements and tried by a fierce attack to make good our failure of the previous night. Captain Matsuoka was first wounded; his thigh was cut away and he could stand no longer. First Lieutenant Miyake was shot through the lungs. The scene went from bad to worse. The Russians behaved as if trying to show that they had been waiting for our coming, proud of their success of the night before. Their search-lights went round so fast as to dazzle our assaulting detachment; their star-lights burned over our heads and made us an easy target for their shooting. "Charge! Forward! Woo-waa!" Thus crying, Captain Yanagawa rushed in most gallantly, in the light of the star-rockets. Half of his face was seen dyed with blood and he was flourishing a glittering sword in his right hand. Again he cried, "Charge!" but that was the last we heard of his brave voice. White blades flashed in the dark, like reeds in the wind, but that flash gradually ceased, the loud yell of a few moments before stopped. We heard only the shouting of the enemy behind their ramparts. They came up and danced for joy on the breastwork, while we had been killed

肉

彈

to create a hill of corpses and a stream of blood! What grief! What sorrow!

Captain Matsuoka, who was seriously wounded as I have said, soon lost so much blood from his wounded thigh, that his breathing became fainter and fainter, and he knew that his end was fast approaching. He pulled out of his pocket the secret maps and destroyed them, and died entangled in the enemy's wire. All who went to fetch him were also killed and went to their eternal sleep side by side with the brave captain. This captain's glorious death was later reported to the Emperor through His Majesty's military chamberlain. That Captain Yanagawa who rushed toward the enemy shouting and yelling, in spite of several wounds, was shot down just at the moment of leaping over the Russian rampart. He leaned against the breastwork of the rampart to die peacefully there after he had done his very best, but the cruel enemy would not allow that. They cut him into pieces and subjected him to wanton cruelties.

Nevertheless, we were determined to deal a heavy blow on some vital part of the enemy, however often and however badly we might be repulsed or routed. We were ready to sacrifice not only a brigade but even a whole division for this important object. Accordingly another great assault was planned for 3 A. M. of the 24th. For several days our company had been bivouacking in the

218

ravine of Yangchia-kou, but now on the night of the 23d we were to leave this place and proceed to the rendezvous of Wuchia-fang. So our captain gathered together his lieutenants and said: —

"Farewell! I have no other words to say to you! I have decided to leave my body on to-morrow's battle-field. Please take this water cup of long separation."

Before these words from our captain we, too, had made up our minds to die this time. We exchanged the farewell cup of water from our water bottle, saying: —

"*This* evening our water tastes like golden nectar!"

Our company quietly left its place of bivouac and fell in under dark willows on the river bank. Thinking that it was the last time we should be together, we could not force back the tears. Soon we began our march and passed on under the dark avenue of trees, where we met a long string of stretchers carrying the wounded who had fallen during the last few days — such a long, almost endless train of stretchers!

"Where are you injured?" I asked one of them as I passed. The wounded man answered, "My legs broken." "Well done! Go quietly."

Our detachment reached the river at the other side of a mountain that looks like the back of an

肉
彈
elephant. It was so dark that we could not see anything at all. We groped our way toward Wu-chia-fang, when in front of us we heard a sound of human voices. I threw myself on the ground and, looking up, saw through the dark that a long line of our wounded were laid down on the river beach. We marched on, sick at heart, over such a tremendous number of the wounded, it took us some time to reach the end of this long line. Their groaning, hard breathing, suffering, pain, their exposure to the night dew without anything to cover them up, was pitiful. We could not help being deeply affected by this scene of misery.

In the meantime we were losing our way, we could not find Wuchia-fang, but suddenly came into the headquarters of the Ninth Division. General Oshima, the commander, was seen clad in his dark winter uniform in spite of the season, a silk crepe *obi* tied tightly about his waist, from which a long Japanese sword was hanging. At the sight of the gallant general we felt as if we were in a region of romance. When his division occupied Panlung, General Oshima is reported to have stood at the head of his army in this dark uniform, making himself the only dark target for the enemy's shot, thus trying to inspire his men with courage and confidence. I asked the way of a staff-officer, and our company turned back in the proper direction. We could not, however, find the right place; we asked again, and were told to go to the right; when we went to the right, we were told to go back to where we started; we were utterly at a loss where to go. The time for our rendezvous was fixed at one o'clock —it was now only a little before that time. If we should fail to appear on the spot in time, it would disgrace us, and we had to think not only of our personal disgrace, but that the prospective attack needed as many fighters as possible. The delay in our arrival might become a cause of defeat. The captain and all of us were extremely anxious and worried. Fortunately, however, at this juncture we came across a man belonging to the engineer-corps, who minutely explained to us how to find Wuchia-fang, telling us to go through the opening a little further on, where our engineers were then engaged in sapping. We went on as instructed and soon found our siege-trenches; we went along these until we came to an opening, beyond which we had to go through the fields exposed to the enemy's view. We ran on, but presently a flash of search-light came! "Lie down!" was ordered, and we waited, holding our breath for that terrible light to disappear. But the search-light would not disappear. Meanwhile communication with our rear was cut off. At last we came to the place which we imagined to be the rendezvous. We found none of our army there, but dark corpses were strewn on the ground. Probably our army

第二十五

肉
彈

had already gathered themselves at the foot of the
East Panlung Fort, which was supposed to be the
centre of our attack. Looking at our watches, we
found that it was a few minutes past one o'clock.
We tried hard to find our main body, but in vain.
Were we too late? The anxiety of our captain was
intense. Our disappointment was agonizing. Were
we to miss our opportunity to join in the general
assault? The captain said, "I cannot expiate my
fault even with suicide!" Not only he, but all of us,
felt that if we failed to join this battle, the company
itself would be disgraced forever; and that compared with that disgrace our unanimous suicide was
a mere trifle.

Scouts were sent in all directions, but none
brought back any news. We had no time to lose,
so we came to the conclusion that the best thing
we could do now was to go to the old fort of East
Panlung and fight even single-handed, and that,
if the main body had begun by that time, we should
be in a good spot to join its action. Thinking that
the occasional sound of a machine-gun that we
had heard must be coming from Panlung, and that
a ravine we had found must lead to that mountain,
we started from Wuchia-fang along the ravine.

Ah, that ravine! a narrow path of less than two
ken in width. It was the place where the Ninth
Division and the Seventh and Ninth Regiments of
the Second Reserve had had such a hard fight the

day before. What a scene of horrors! No stretcher nor medicine chest could be brought there. The dead and wounded were piled one upon another in nooks and corners, some groaning with pain, some crying for help, and some perfectly quiet, breathing no longer. We hardly found space to walk without stepping on them. It was an infernal tunnel of the dead and dying. We groped to the right not to step on a dead comrade, only to kick a wounded one on the left. Where we stepped, thinking that it was on mother earth, we found ourselves walking over the khaki-colored dead. "Don't step on the corpses!" I shouted to my men; but at that very moment I was treading on the chest of one. "Pardon," was the only apology I could offer the dead thus unintentionally insulted. Along this long, narrow path full of corpses, it was impossible not to step on our poor, silent comrades.

We were almost at the end of the ravine — a few steps more would have brought us face to face with wire-entanglements — when we stopped short for a while. All at once the enemy's machine-guns began at our left, shooting out flames of fire through the dark. Presently we heard the noise of a gun detachment; six of our guns were trying to climb Panlung through the same ravine. In this narrow pass the infantry and artillery men were jumbled together to escape the fire of the Russian machine-guns.

肉

彈

We were now at the foot of the objective mountain, but no trace of the main body could be found.
What a disappointment and pain for us! Where
was it? Was the expected assault postponed? After
a great deal of cogitation the captain decided to
go back to Wuchia-fang and wait for further orders.
This was his deliberately formed conclusion, and
of course we had to obey him, though very reluctantly. Once again we must go through that infernal tunnel. Those corpses of the dead comrades
on which we had stepped and to which we had
apologized in horror had to be trodden on once
more. We looked for the dead and wounded in the
dark and found their condition still worse and more
miserable than before, because the artillery-men
had been through the same place after us, and
many dead and dying had been run over by the
gun carriages. Those who had been breathing
faintly had breathed their last under the iron wheels;
those who had already died were cut to pieces.
Shattered bones, torn flesh, flowing blood, were
mingled with broken swords and split rifles. What
could be more shocking than this scene!

We went back to the entrance of the ravine and
waited there for a while; at last group after group
of shadows began to come through the dark. It
was our main body! Our joy was unbounded. We
learned that they had not been able to reach the
place of rendezvous at the appointed hour, on ac-

count of the constant hindrance to their march offered by the enemy's search-lights. We breathed a
sigh of relief in thus joining the main body at last,
and rejoiced over the prospect of forming with
them the advance guard of the first general assault.
This place of gathering did not shield us from the
enemy's fire, nor was it large enough to accommo-
date a great number of men; it was only protected
by a precipice that would prevent the enemy from
looking down upon us. Among the officers who
were with us here was Major Matsumura, who distinguished himself at Taku-shan after its capture
by our army by resisting and repulsing the enemy's
counter-attack. He had sprained his right foot at
that time, but would not consent to receive medical
treatment for such a trifling injury as he called it,
and was still doing the duty of a battalion commander. This night he was still suffering from his
foot; but supporting himself with a willow stick,
he walked on at the head of his battalion. Sitting
down beside me, he said, "The time it has come
at last!"

Captain Segawa, who bade that sad farewell to
his younger brother at Taku-shan, was also there.
Lieutenant Sone came along with a cartridge belt
round his waist and a rifle in his hand. I asked him
why he was so strangely armed. Upon which he
said that he had lost his sword during the scouting
of the previous night and had therefore armed him-

self like a private soldier. All the officers gathered together wished each other success and chatted cheerfully for a while. Only a few hours later, all of them had been killed except Major Matsumura and myself! Whenever I think of it, I still feel as if I saw their faces and heard their voices. Brave fellows! Poor men! My heart is full of strange emotions when I think of them.

第
二
十
六

THE FORLORN HOPE

WE all fell in under the precipice and were waiting for the order of march, when a piece of paper reached me handed from man to man. I opened it and read: —

"Yasukichi Honda was shot on the 19th, and when I offered him a drink of water he shed tears and asked me to give his compliments to Lieutenant Sakurai.

(Signed) "BUNKICHI TAKEO."

This Honda had been my servant about a year before, and he was a faithful fellow. His last words were a farewell to me who had done so little for him. I was deeply affected by his loyal devotion. Even now I regret I had no chance of giving him a farewell hand-shake, and cannot help thinking how greatly he would have rejoiced if I could have given him one word of good-by while he was yet alive.

I gathered my men around me and said: "I now bid you all farewell. Fight with all your might. This

肉
彈

battle will decide whether Port Arthur is to fall or not. This water you drink, please drink as if at your death moment."

I filled a cup with water that was fetched by one or two soldiers at the risk of their lives, and we all drank farewell from the same cup. Soon we received orders to advance to a point half-way up the side of Panlung. We began to move on quietly; we who had already drunk together the death-cup went again through that same terrible ravine full of our dead comrades. This was the third time that we had traveled by this path, and none expected to walk over it a fourth time alive. To die under the flying Flag of the Rising Sun, and to die while doing splendid service to one's country, was the wish and resolve of every heart. Before beginning this final march to the battle-field, we all made ourselves as light as possible; we carried with us just enough hard biscuit, "iron rations," to support life for two or three days; the rest we left behind. My khaki uniform was decorated by a national flag hanging from my belt, a Japanese towel was tied around my neck. I wore no shoes, only tabi[1] on my feet, and my whole appearance was like that of a dancer at a summer festival in Tokyo. I carried with me my sword, my water bottle, and three hard biscuit. Thus armed and

[1] *Tabi*, the Japanese sock, made with a separate place for the great toe.

attired I was to appear on the glorious stage of death.

The mere thought of this ravine makes one shudder even now. We jumped over or stepped on the heaped-up corpses and went on holding our noses. What a grief it was to have to tread on the bodies of our heroic dead! I found one wounded man squatting in a corner groaning with pain. I asked him where he was wounded. He told me that his legs were broken, and for three days he had had no single grain of rice, nor a single drop of water; no stretcher had appeared, and he had been waiting for the arrival of death ever since he fought and fell. I gave him the three biscuit I had, and told him to eat those and wait patiently for the coming of our bearer company. He clasped his hands together and shed tears for joy and gratitude and begged me to tell him my name. I was deeply touched by this experience. "Farewell" was the only thing I could say to the poor fellow as I passed on. We now came to the wire-entanglement of Panlung-shan.

This fortress of Panlung had been captured with the flesh and blood of the Ninth Division and the Seventh and Eighth Regiments of the Second Reserve, and was now an important base from which a general assault on the northern forts of East Kikuan and Wantai was to be made. This critical spot was finally taken after a terrible struggle and a valiant

肉彈

action by the men of General Oshima's command. The sad story was eloquently told by the horrible sights of the ravine. While running through the opening in the wire-entanglement beyond, I noticed many engineers and infantry-men dead, piled one upon another, caught in the wire, or taking hold with both arms of a post, or grasping the iron shears.

When we reached the middle of the side of Pan-lung, I saw the regimental flag that I used to carry, flying above our heads in the dark. My heart leaped at the sight of the dear flag. I scrambled up to where it was planted and came face to face with Colonel Aoki, with whom I had exchanged fare-well salutations at the foot of Taku-shan some days before.

"Colonel, I am Lieutenant Sakurai!"

He looked at me as if thinking fondly of bygone days, and said:—

"Are you Sakurai? I do pray for your success."

After this word from my commander, how could I be satisfied without doing something? I must exert myself to the uttermost.

Then I heard a voice calling my name from the top of the mountain, so I bade farewell to the colonel and went on to the top to find Lieutenant Yoshida, a friend of mine from the same province, sitting there alone. I had heard of his being in the Ninth Division, fighting before Port Arthur, but I did not expect ever to meet him. To see an old friend just before going into a fierce engagement was touching.

"Sakurai, is n't it fearful, the fighting of the last few days?"

Wondering why he was there, I asked: "What are you doing here alone?"

"Please look at these corpses!"

There were dark shadows about him which I had thought were the recruits of our regiment. I could not help being astonished when I found that those heaps of khaki-colored men were the dead or wounded soldiers of Lieutenant Yoshida's command. What a horrible sight! Their bodies were piled up two or three or even four deep; some had died with their hands on the enemy's battery, some had successfully gone beyond the battery and were killed grasping the gun-carriages. A sad groaning came from the wounded who were buried under the dead. When this gallant assaulting column had pressed upon the enemy's forts, stepping over their comrades' bodies, the terrible and skillful fire of the machine-guns had killed them all, close by the forts, piling the dead upon the wounded. The men behind, angry at their comrades' death, attempted a summary revenge, but they rushed upon the enemy only to swell the number of the dead, and Lieutenant Yoshida felt that he could not leave his unfortunate men, and was watching over their remains with a breaking heart. Later, on the

肉
彈

27th of October, he fought most desperately at Erhlung and died. This interview at the top of Panlung was our last good-by.

As soon as we were gathered together the colonel rose and gave us a final word of exhortation, saying: "This battle is our great chance of serving our country. To-night we must strike at the vitals of Port Arthur. Our brave assaulting column must be not simply a forlorn-hope ('resolved-to-die'), but a 'sure-death' detachment. I as your father am more grateful than I can express for your gallant fighting. Do your best, all of you."

Yes, we were all ready for death when leaving Japan. Men going to battle of course cannot expect to come back alive. But in this particular battle to be ready for death was not enough; what was required of us was a determination not to fail to die. Indeed, we were "sure-death" men, and this new appellation gave us a great stimulus. Also a telegram that had come from the Minister of War in Tokyo, was read by the aide-de-camp, which said, "I pray for your success." This increased the exaltation of our spirits.

Let me now recount the sublimity and horror of this general assault. I was a mere lieutenant and everything passed through my mind as in a dream, so my story must be something like picking out things from the dark. I can't give you any systematic account, but must limit myself to fragmentary recollections. If this story sounds like a vain-glorious account of my own achievements, it is not because I am conscious of my merit when I have so little to boast of, but because the things concerning me and near me are what I can tell you with authority. If this partial account prove a clue from which the whole story of this terrible assault may be inferred, my work will not have been in vain.

The men of the "sure-death" detachment rose to their part. Fearlessly they stepped forward to the place of death. They went over Panlung-shan and made their way through the piled-up bodies of the dead, groups of five or six soldiers reaching the barricaded slope one after another.

I said to the colonel, "Good-by, then!"

With this farewell I started, and my first step was on the head of a corpse. Our objective points were the Northern Fortress and Wang-tai Hill.

There was a fight with bombs at the enemy's skirmish-trenches. The bombs sent from our side exploded finely, and the place became at once a conflagration, boards were flung about, sand bags burst, heads flew around, legs were torn off. The flames mingled with the smoke, lighted up our faces weirdly, with a red glare, and all at once the battle-line became confused. Then the enemy, thinking it hopeless, left the place and began to flee. "Forward! forward! Now is the time to go forward! Forward! Pursue! Capture it with one

肉
弾

bound!" and, proud of our victory, we went forward, courageously.

Captain Kawakami, raising his sword, cried, "Forward!" and then I, standing close by him, cried, "Sakurai's company, forward!"

Thus shouting I left the captain's side, and, in order to see the road we were to follow, went behind the rampart. What is that black object which obstructs our view? It is the ramparts of the Northern Fortress. Looking back, I did not see a soldier. Alack, had the line been cut? In trepidation, keeping my body to the left for safety, I called the Twelfth Company.

"Lieutenant Sakurai!" a voice called out repeatedly in answer. Returning in the direction of the sound, I found Corporal Ito weeping loudly.

"What are you crying for? What has happened?"

The corporal, weeping bitterly, gripped my arm tightly.

"Lieutenant Sakurai, you have become an important person."

"What is there to weep about? I say, what is the matter?"

He whispered in my ear, "Our captain is dead."

Hearing this, I too wept. Was it not only a moment ago that he had given the order "Forward"? Was it not even now that I had separated from him? And yet our captain was one of the dead. In one moment our tender, pitying Captain Kawakami and I had become beings of two separate worlds. Was it a dream or a reality, I wondered?

Corporal Ito pointed out the captain's body, which had fallen inside the rampart only a few rods away. I hastened thither and raised him in my arms.

"Captain!" I could not say a word more.

But as matters could not remain thus, I took the secret map which the captain had, and, rising up boldly, called out, "From henceforward I command the Twelfth Company." And I ordered that some one of the wounded should carry back the captain's corpse. A wounded soldier was just about to raise it up when he was struck on a vital spot and died leaning on the captain. One after another of the soldiers who took his place was struck and fell.

I called Sub-Lieutenant Ninomiya and asked him if the sections were together.

He answered in the affirmative. I ordered Corporal Ito not to let the line be cut, and told him that I would be in the centre of the skirmishers. In the darkness of the night we could not distinguish the features of the country, nor in which direction we were to march. Standing up abruptly against the dark sky were the Northern Fortress and Wang-tai Hill. In front of us lay a natural stronghold, and we were in a caldron-shaped hollow. But still we marched on side by side.

235

"The Twelfth Company forward!"

I turned to the right and went forward as in a dream. I remember nothing clearly of the time.

"Keep the line together!"

This was my one command. Presently I ceased to hear the voice of Corporal Ito, who had been at my right hand. The bayonets gleaming in the darkness became fewer. The black masses of soldiers who had pushed their way on now became a handful. All at once, as if struck by a club, I fell down sprawling on the ground. I was wounded, struck in my right hand. The splendid magnesium light of the enemy flashed out, showing the piled-up bodies of the dead, and I raised my wounded hand and looked at it. It was broken at the wrist; the hand hung down and was bleeding profusely. I took out the already loosened bundle of bandages,[1] tied up my wound with the triangular piece, and then wrapping a handkerchief over it, I slung it from my neck with the sunrise flag, which I had sworn to plant on the enemy's fortress.

Looking up, I saw that only a valley lay between me and Wang-tai Hill, which almost touched the sky. I wished to drink and sought at my waist, but the canteen was gone; its leather strap alone was entangled in my feet. The voices of the soldiers were lessening one by one. In contrast, the glare

[1] The "first aid" bandages, prepared by the Red Cross Society, issued to every soldier as part of his equipment.

236

of the rockets of the hated enemy and the frightful noise of the cannonading increased. I slowly rubbed my legs, and, seeing that they were unhurt, I again rose. Throwing aside the sheath of my sword, I carried the bare blade in my left hand as a staff, went down the slope as in a dream, and climbed Wang-tai Hill.

The long and enormously heavy guns were towering before me, and how few of my men were left alive now! I shouted and told the survivors to follow me, but few answered my call. When I thought that the other detachments must also have been reduced to a similar condition, my heart began to fail me. No reinforcement was to be hoped for, so I ordered a soldier to climb the rampart and plant the sun flag overhead, but alas! he was shot and killed, without even a sound or cry.

All of a sudden a stupendous sound as from another world rose around about me.

"Counter-assault!"

A detachment of the enemy appeared on the rampart, looking like a dark wooden barricade. They surrounded us in the twinkling of an eye and raised a cry of triumph. Our disadvantageous position would not allow us to offer any resistance, and our party was too small to fight them. We had to fall back down the steep hill. Looking back, I saw the Russians shooting at us as they pursued. When we reached the earthworks before mentioned, we made a stand and faced the enemy. Great confusion and infernal butchery followed. Bayonets clashed against bayonets; the enemy brought out machine-guns and poured shot upon us pell-mell; the men on both sides fell like grass. But I cannot give you a detailed account of the scene, because I was then in a dazed condition. I only remember that I was brandishing my sword in fury. I also felt myself occasionally cutting down the enemy. I remember a confused fight of white blade against white blade, the rain and hail of shell, a desperate fight here and a confused scuffle there. At last I grew so hoarse that I could not shout any more. Suddenly my sword broke with a clash, my left arm was pierced. I fell, and before I could rise a shell came and shattered my right leg. I gathered all my strength and tried to stand up, but I felt as if I were crumbling and fell to the ground perfectly powerless. A soldier who saw me fall cried, "Lieutenant Sakurai, let us die together."

I embraced him with my left arm and, gnashing my teeth with regret and sorrow, I could only watch the hand-to-hand fight going on about me. My mind worked like that of a madman, but my body would not move an inch.

第二十七

LIFE OUT OF DEATH

THE day of the 24th of August dawned upon a battle-ground covered with the dead and wounded of both sides. I discovered that the man in my arms was Kensuke Ono, a soldier whom I had trained. He was wounded in the right eye and pierced through the side. Thinking that he could not live, he had called my name and offered to die with me. Poor, dear fellow! My left arm that embraced him was covered with dark red clots of blood, which was running over Ono's neck. Ono removed my arm, quietly pulled out his bandages, and bound up my left arm. Thus I lay surrounded by the enemy and seriously wounded; there seemed no slightest hope of my escape. If I did not expire then, it was certain that I should soon be in the enemy's hands, which meant a misfortune far more intolerable than death. My heart yearned to commit suicide before such a disgrace should befall me, but I had no weapon with me, no hand that could help me in the act. Tears of regret choked me.

239

肉
彈

"Ono, please kill me and go back and report the conditions," I urged him. I begged him to kill me, but he would not consent. He was almost blind, for both his eyes were covered with blood, but he grasped his rifle and said, "I resist your orders."

I expostulated with him and explained our position, saying that the enemy had changed their attitude to a counter-attack and we were already surrounded by them; beside that, we had gone far into the enemy's ground since the previous night, so that if we remained in that helpless state we were sure of being made prisoners. Then I asked him how he felt about becoming a captive of the Russians, and told him that it was a far greater mercy to me who could not move a limb for him to kill me at once and make good his escape. But Ono was already losing his reason and simply continued saying, "I resist your orders." There was no other help, and I resigned myself to dying where I was. At the same time I was extremely anxious to send Ono and let him report the condition of affairs at the present moment. So as a means to make him go I said, "Bring me a stretcher and I will go," and urged him to hurry up. Of course I knew full well that, since that incarnation of love in the shape of a stretcher company could not reach the ravine, much less could it come to this spot encircled by the enemy, my only hope was that he might thus have a chance of returning alive to our main body and also of reporting my death. Ono, in a state of frenzy, jumped up at my words, and saying, "Please wait here," ran over to the earthworks and disappeared. Would he successfully go through the enemy's investment, back to our main position? Later, when I found him in a hospital, I was astonished at his good fortune.

I was thus left lying alone surrounded by dead and dying. This moment was the most hallowed, the most painfully sad, and the most exasperating in my life. I repeated to myself Nelson's words, "Thank heaven, I have done my duty!" and comforted myself with the idea that, though doomed to failure, I had done my whole life's work. I thought of nothing else. I was only conscious that the life-blood of a man twenty-five years of age was fast flowing to its speedy exhaustion, but did not feel the pain of the wounds at all. A number of the Russians were going to and fro in the trenches only a few *ken* from me and firing at our surviving men, each Russian using five or six rifles in turn. While I was watching their action with wide-open eyes, one of them turned back and noticed my being still alive. He signaled to the others, and three or four shots visited me at once. They fixed their bayonets and came jumping toward me. I shut my eyes. I was about to be butchered. My body was not of iron and stone to begin with, and its

limbs were shattered and had no power to resist
or chase the enemy. I could not escape from the
poisonous teeth of the wolves. But Providence had
not forsaken me yet. At this critical moment I only
heard the din of a close fight near me, but was
spared the point of an unknown savage's bayonet.
As they rushed toward me, five or six of our survivors encountered them, fought them, and all
fell. And I who had had nothing but sure death
to wait for was saved at the cost of my poor comrades' lives. By this sacrifice was my faint breathing
continued.

At this juncture a man jumped up the earthworks with a loud yell, and his sword raised high
in the air. Who was this brave fellow who stormed
the enemy's trenches single-handed? I was astonished at his audacity. But alas! a shot came flying
from somewhere, hit him, and he fell at my right
side, as if crumbling down. He faced death as if
returning home. He had jumped up there bravely
all alone to seek death, and attracted the enemy's
attention by his triumphant cry.

After a while the shells from the Japanese army
began to burst briskly above our heads. Percus-
sion balls fell around us and hurled up smoke and
blood together. Legs, hands, and necks were cut
into black fragments, and scattered about. I shut
my eyes in perfect resignation and prayed that my
agony might be put to a speedy end by my being

shattered to pieces all at once. Still no shell came to break my flesh and bones, but only small fragments came and injured my already wounded limbs. One wounded soldier who was near me received one of those horrible fragments on the face. He writhed for a few minutes, then fell on his face and expired. Every moment I expected to meet a similar fate; or to be eaten by the hungry dogs and wolves of the field, half dead, half alive, yet unable to resist my fate. I was being picked off inch by inch by the fierce eagle of the north. I heard some one crying "Nippon Banzai" at my head. I opened my eyes and dimly discovered that is was a poor, wounded man. His reason was all gone, yet he did not forget to shout Banzai for his Fatherland. He repeated Banzai over and over again, and also shouted "Come, come, Japanese soldiers!" He danced, jumped, and shouted in frenzy until he was exhausted, then he closed his lips and his color began to fade. I shut my eyes and prayed that he might go in peace.

The blood from my wounds had dyed my body red all over. My arms were bandaged, but all the other wounds were left uncovered. Sometimes I shut my eyes in quiet thought and again opened them to stare about me. To my left I saw two Japanese soldiers lying dead under the flying Rising Sun. Probably the flag had been planted there by these two heroes, but if our men pushed forward to it, the enemy were sure to shoot them down; while, if the Russians attempted to retake the spot, they were equally sure of being killed by our artillery. This dauntless pair had kept the spot unto death, and they must have died smiling and contented at their success. Is this not a fine piece of poetry in itself? What poet will sing these heroes to posterity!

As I was faintly smiling over this poetic sight of the battle-field, I saw the most brutal act committed that I could have imagined. Ah, men and women of a civilization of justice and mercy, please remember this fact! I have already told you of a savage Russian who butchered Captain Yanagawa wantonly. Here again, before my very eyes, I saw a Russian commit a most deliberate act of cruelty and barbarism. I had noticed a Russian officer repeatedly pointing to his wounded leg and making signs with his hands for help. Later I saw a Japanese hospital orderly, himself wounded, go up to the Russian. Without attending to his own wound, he took out bandages from a bag at his waist and bandaged the Russian. He did his duty of love and mercy faithfully, thinking that the wounded foe was not a foe any more, only a hero who had toiled for his own country. His kindness in dressing the wound of the Russian was so beautiful and holy that tearful gratitude was due to him even from a hard-hearted savage. But how did this

Russian return the kindness of this hospital orderly? Tears of gratitude? No! A hand-shake of thanks? No! Indeed, no! Lo, this beastly Russian officer bestowed a pistol shot upon his Japanese benefactor! Do not forget this, you people of justice and humanity! As soon as the orderly had finished bandaging, the Russian pulled out his revolver from his hip and took the life of the good Samaritan with one shot! My heart was bursting with indignation at the sight of this atrocious outrage!

But my indignation, my exasperation, could not be translated into action. I simply shut my eyes and gnashed my teeth; soon my breathing became difficult. I felt that my life was fast ebbing, when some one caught hold of my coat and raised me; after a minute I was let alone. I slightly opened my eyes and dimly saw two or three Russians going up the hill. I had been on the point of being made a prisoner! That very moment when I was raised and laid down was the boundary-line between my life and death, between my honor and disgrace! The enemy caught hold of me once, but soon let me go; probably they thought I was dead. No wonder they thought so, for I was covered with blood.

Then some one came running stealthily to my side and fell down without a word. Was he dead? No, he was simply feigning death. After a while he whispered in my ear: "Let us go back. I will help you."

第二十七

肉
彈

In the midst of my panting, irregular breathing, I looked at the man. He was a stranger to me, a private with his head bandaged. I replied to his very kind offer and said that I could never get back alive under the circumstances, and wished him to kill me and go himself if he could. He said that he could not expect to get me back alive, but that he would at least carry my body; he would not allow it to be left among the enemy. As soon as he had said this, he caught my left arm and put it on his shoulder. At this juncture, the brave fellow who was lying at my right, and who had been groaning for some time, said in a faltering, tearful voice:—

"Lieutenant, please give me the last cup of water." My heart was bursting with emotion, and I fell down by his side in spite of my helper. This poor fellow was probably one of my men; he asked me to send him out on his last journey. Poor, poor soul! Of course I could not force myself to go and leave my poor comrade alone.

"Have you any water?" I asked my helper. Whereupon he took out his water bottle, stepped over my chest, and poured water into the mouth of the dying man, who put his shattered hands together as in supplication and murmuring "Namu-Amida-Butsu![1] Namu-Amida-Butsu!" like a faint echo, slowly drew his last breath.

I had no heart to leave behind other comrades,

[1] "I adore thee, O Eternal Buddha!"

dead or wounded, and seek my own safety. But
my kind helper grasped my left arm once again,
raised me on his back, and in one bound leaped
over the earthwork, when both of us went down
with a thud. Quickly he picked up an overcoat
and covered me with it, and again in silence lay
down by my side. In this way I was taken out of
the trenches on the back of an unknown soldier.
It was while being thus carried that my legs touched
a corner of the earthwork, and I felt excruciating
pain for the first time. After a while he whispered
to me again, "As the shot are coming fast now, we
must wait a little." He unsheathed his bayonet and
bound it as a splint to my broken leg with a Japanese towel. I was very thirsty and wanted to drink;
he gave me all that was left in his bottle, saying,
"Don't drink much." And also he soothed me often,
saying, "Please be patient awhile." I saw many
comrades groaning and writhing about me, and my
kind helper would pick up water bottles scattered
over the place and give them drink. Often he
would feign death to escape the enemy's eyes, and
lie down quickly, covering me with his body. I did
not yet know even the name of this chivalrous man.

"What is your name?" I asked.

"My name is Takesaburo Kondo," he answered,
in a whisper.

"Which regiment?"

"I am in the Kochi regiment."

I was being saved by a gallant soldier, who was neither my subordinate, nor of the same regiment as myself, and whom I had never seen before. What mysterious thread of fortune bound him and me together? I could not explain the mystery, but I do know that it was the friendly, brotherly spirit pervading all ranks of our army that produced such a man as Kondo, whose name should be handed down to posterity as a model soldier and a heroic character. A few hours after I had been rescued, I fell into a state of complete unconsciousness. When at last I recovered my senses, the first thing that came to my mind was the beloved name of Kondo.

Brave Takesaburo! He not only rescued me from the encircling enemy of Wantai, but also with great difficulty carried me to our main position. It was daytime and the place was exposed to the Russian machine-guns. He himself was wounded. If he had left me there, me whose life was more than uncertain, and escaped to a safe place by himself, things would have been much simpler for him. But he had sworn to help me, and that promise was more important to him than his own life. He braved every danger, bore every difficulty, and with wonderful tact and sagacity made use of every possible device in my rescue, and he was under no personal obligation to me. For a while he covered and protected me with his body, then he said to me:—

"Although a great many shot are still falling about us, we must not stay here till night, or the enemy are sure to come and kill us. We must go now. Please consider yourself already dead."

He wrapped me up with an overcoat and beckoned to another soldier near by. The wounded man came crawling to my side and, when he saw me, said:—

"Are you not Lieutenant Sakurai?"

I did not know who he was, but he must have been of the same regiment as myself, since he knew me. He said to me, "How badly you are injured!" and whispered with Takesaburo. Then I was carried away by these two men and left behind me Wantai, now the grave of the unconsoled spirits of my dear comrades, thinking all the time that it was a great shame to go back alone, leaving the dead and wounded friends behind. My two helpers would lie down every five or ten steps as if they were dead, and try to deceive the enemy's vigilance. While being thus carried I felt no pain, only a very unpleasant grating of broken bones. We went past wire-entanglements and breastworks, and in the burning, straight, noonday rays of the sun, I was finally brought to a ravine a little below the wire-entanglement, and I thought the place was the foot of Kikuan.

I was laid down here for some time, and at last began to feel faint and dizzy, and everything went out of my consciousness as in sleep. This was caused by the profuse bleeding. At this time I was counted among the dead; the report of my death reached home. My teacher, Mr. Murai, placed the postal card I had written to him in the family shrine[1] and offered to my spirit incense and flowers, as I have since been told.

For some hours I was practically dead in this ravine, but the gate of the other world was still closed against me and I began to breathe once more. The first thing that I heard was a tremendous noise of a heavy cannon-ball falling near me, throwing up sand and pebbles, and covering me with dust.

I felt that it was this roar that called my spirit back into this world. As soon as I recovered consciousness, my wounds began to hurt terribly. I tried to move my comparatively sound right leg, but it would not move; the blood gushed out of it and coagulated over it. I noticed that a sun flag was spread over my face as an awning and that Takesaburo Kondo was still by my side watching me. I thanked him for his faithful service with tears of gratitude.

He fastened poles to the overcoat wrapping me and begged four or five wounded men who happened to come along to help carry me to the first aid. Lifting a corner of the flag that covered my face, he said: "Lieutenant, it seems that my wound

---

[1] The "Buddha Shelf," the shrine in the house where are kept the tablets of the dead.

is not a serious one, as I am not going to the rear. Your case is serious. Please take good care of yourself and become well again," and he left me at last. I never saw him again.

Did I take his hand and thank him for his gallant service? No; I could not. I only wept for his goodness with unbounded gratitude in my heart and prayed that he might be spared. "To share the shadow of the same tree, to drink from the same stream of water," is said to be the promise of meeting again in another world. But he voluntarily threw himself into the boiling caldron of danger and rescued me out of certain death; he was truly the giver of my renewed life. My present life is not mine at all; I should have died in Bodai surely: that I now live is due to Takesaburo Kondo alone. Kondo was killed within a month after this! His spirit is now too far away to see me, whom he rescued amid such great difficulties and dangers. When I think of this I cannot cry out my sorrow or talk about my sentiments, because both the cry and the words become choked in my throat.

During the night four or five wounded soldiers took advantage of the darkness to carry me past the enemy's front to the first aid, which they found with difficulty. I was still faint and in a dreamy state and could not take in much; the only thing I remember is that I was put on a stretcher, without removing overcoat and poles on which I had been

第二十七

borne thus far. At last I was laid down in a spot where people were busy running to and fro. That was indeed the first aid station. As soon as I realized this, I cried out: —

"Is Surgeon Yasui here? Surgeon Ando?"

"I am Ando! Yasui is also here!" was the immediate response. I did not expect to find these friends here, but simply called their names as in a dream, the names so dear to my heart. But the strange, mysterious thread that tied us together in friendship drew me to their place and put me under their care — a thing that could never be planned or mapped out in the battle-field, where separation and dispersion is so universal a rule. Heaven granted me a chance to meet them in my time of need. At this unexpected hearing of their voices my heart beat high.

"Surgeon Yasui! Surgeon Ando!"

They took my hands and stroked my forehead and said: "Well done. You have done well."

I noticed that the body of my battalion commander, Major Kamimura, was lying to my left. When attacking the first skirmish-trenches, he was standing in the farthest front and cheering us on. And that same brave officer was now a spiritless corpse sleeping an eternal sleep here, his servant clinging to his body, crying at the top of his voice.

Soon I was bandaged and sent to the rear, and had to say an unwilling farewell to the two surgeon friends whom I had come across to my unexpected and unbounded joy!

When I met Surgeon Yasui later, he told me something of my condition at the time I was taken to the first aid: —

"The position of that first aid station was such that none of us expected to find any of the wounded of our detachment brought there; yet I was enabled to take care of you; that is the strangest of strange happenings. I had asked about you of the wounded men as they came in, and all said that you must be dead. There was one even who affirmed that you were killed below the wire-entanglements of Kikuan. So I had concluded that I should never see you again in this world of the living, but wishing to recover your body, I made careful inquiries about where you were killed — all to no purpose. Later, a sergeant by the name of Sadaoka came in, and I asked him about you and got the answer that you had been killed in the ravine of Kikuan. At once I dispatched some hospital orderlies to bring your body back on a stretcher, but it was too dark, and the enemy's fire was still violent, and they came back without accomplishing anything. Still anxious to get you, I sent out a second group of orderlies, who brought you back, still living, to our great surprise and joy. At the first glance we thought that you must die in a few hours, and Surgeon Ando and I looked at each other in sorrow. Therefore, when we sent you on to the field hospital, of course we thought it was an eternal good-by in disguise.

"About a month after that I saw Takesaburo Kondo, who had rescued you, and a strange coincidence it was. I noticed a soldier passing our first aid station, shouldering a shovel. Suddenly the man fell face upward. I ran to the spot and saw that it was your Takesaburo Kondo. He was a special object of my respect and love, because I knew that he had saved you out of the enemy's grip. He was still breathing faintly, so I gave him a drink from my water bottle; then he smiled and expired in peace."

Thus the giver of my second life, Takesaburo Kondo, lost his noble life by a stray shot!

Our first general attack came to a close with these horrors. The second and the third repeated similar scenes or even more horrible ones. But our army was not discouraged; on the contrary, the repeated failures only added to their keen determination and abundant resourcefulness. Our army attacked again and again the desperately defending enemy, and at last took the great fortress. I have no right to speak about the investment of Port Arthur after this first assault. There are others better fitted to relate that great chapter of the war. For about three hundred days after this I was kept in bed, unable to move my hands or to stand on my feet. But in the agony of physical pain I was running to Liaotung in imagination, picturing to myself the brave and loyal officers and men fighting gallantly in the field. And on the second day of the Happy New Year of the 38th of Meiji I heard the news that the great fortress of Port Arthur, considered the strongest east of Suez, and the formidable base for the Russian policy of the aggression on Eastern Asia, no longer able to resist the tremendous power of the Imperial forces, had capitulated, and its commanding general had given himself up to the mercy of General Nogi. When I heard this news, not only I, but all the wounded who had taken part in the siege, wept while we rejoiced. The bleached white bones of our brave dead that filled the hills and valleys of Port Arthur must have risen and danced with joy! The spirits of those loyal ones who died unconsoled, crying "Revenge!" or "Port Arthur!" must have been lulled to eternal rest by this great news.

When I heard of the capitulation of Port Arthur, I cried with an overwhelming joy, and at the same time there came to me the thought of the great number of my dead comrades. I who had had the misfortune of sacrificing the lives of so many of my men on the battle-field, how could I apologize to their loyal spirits? I who left many brethren on the field and came back alone to save my life, how could I see without shame the faces of their surviving relatives?

The war is now over, the storm has ceased! The blood of brave warriors has bought this peace. The time may come when the hills of Port Arthur are razed to the ground and the river of Liaotung is dried up, but the time will never come when the names of the hundreds of thousands of those loyal officers and patriotic soldiers who gave their lives to the sovereign and to the country will be forgotten. Their names shall be fragrant for a thousand years and lighten ten thousand ages; their merits posterity shall gratefully remember for ever and ever!

APPENDICES

APPENDIX A

THE IMPERIAL RESCRIPT ON EDUCATION

KNOW ye, Our subjects:

Our Imperial Ancestors have founded Our Empire on a basis broad and everlasting and have deeply and firmly implanted virtue; Our subjects ever united in loyalty and filial piety have from generation to generation illustrated the beauty thereof. This is the glory of the fundamental character of Our Empire, and herein also lies the source of Our education. Ye, Our subjects, be filial to your parents, affectionate to your brothers and sisters; as husbands and wives be harmonious, as friends true; bear yourselves in modesty and moderation; extend your benevolence to all; pursue learning and cultivate arts, and thereby develop intellectual faculties and perfect moral powers; furthermore advance public good and promote common interests; always respect the Constitution and observe the laws; should emergency arise, offer yourselves courageously to the State; and thus guard and maintain the prosperity of Our Imperial Throne coeval with heaven and earth. So shall ye not only be Our good and faithful subjects, but render illustrious the best traditions of your forefathers.

The way here set forth is indeed the teaching bequeathed by Our Imperial Ancestors, to be observed alike by Their Descendants and subjects, infallible for all ages and true in all places. It is Our wish to lay it to heart in all reverence, in common with you, Our subjects, that we may all thus attain to the same virtue.

The 30th day of the 10th month of the 23d year of Meiji.

[Imperial Sign Manual. Imperial Seal.]

APPENDIX B

IMPERIAL RESCRIPT TO THE ARMY AND NAVY

THE Army of this country, in ancient times, stood from generation to generation under the supreme command of the Emperor. More than two thousand five hundred years have passed since the time when the Emperor Jimmu suppressed the barbarian tribes of the central provinces, and established himself on his Imperial Throne. The expedition was under the supreme command of the Emperor himself, and was composed of warriors of Otomo and Mononobe, the most illustrious warrior-clans of the day.

Military reorganization often was necessitated in subsequent ages by the vicissitudes of the times and the needs of the country's wars; but throughout Our ancient history, the Emperor was always the regular commander. His place in the field was sometimes taken by the queen or the crown prince, but the supreme command of the Army was never intrusted to a subject.

In the Middle Ages all administrative matters, whether military or civil, were copied from China: six garrisons were organized, and two depots for horses, and a system of frontier guards were likewise established. The organization of the army was thus excellent on paper; but the long continuance of peace ruined the efficiency of the army, farmers and soldiers became two distinct classes.

The warriors imperceptibly changed into a professional caste, popularly called *bushi*, the principal men of which became the permanent leaders of the army; and the general chaos of the national life placed the chief powers of the Government in their hands, and kept them there for close upon seven hundred years.

No human power could probably have arrested this turn of Our national life; and yet it was a thing much to be regretted as being entirely out of harmony with Our national constitution and the rules laid down by Our ancestors.

After the periods of Kokwa (A. D. 1844) and Ka-ei (A. D. 1848) the Government of the Tokugawa House became too feeble to bear the responsibilities of national government, and a critical period was made more critical by the petitions for admission and intercourse which came from foreign nations. These circumstances caused great anxiety to Our Grandfather, the Emperor Ninko, and Our Father, the late Emperor Komei. When, not long afterwards, We ascended the throne in Our youth, the Shogun Tokugawa returned his authority into Our hands, and the lesser Barons likewise restored to Us their territories. Thus, in less than one year, the whole country came once more under Our direct control, and We were thus enabled to restore again the old system of Government. This great result was due in part to the meritorious services of Our loyal subjects of all classes who aided Us in the accomplishment of this great work, and partly to the mercy which every Emperor of this country has felt for Our people; but the basis of the whole work now successfully accomplished has been the fact that Our people themselves have a just knowledge of right and wrong and rightly apprehend the meaning of true loyalty.

During the fifteen years that have elapsed since then, We have reorganized Our military and naval system, and formed Our present army and navy in order to make Our country glorious. The army and navy is now under Our direct command, and though partial commands may from time to time be intrusted to some of Our subjects, the supreme command will always remain with Us. We desire you to remember this fact, and to let your descendants know that the Emperor is Commander-in-Chief of the Army and Navy, so that the country may never again have to go through the ignominy of the Middle Ages.

We are your Commander-in-Chief and as such We rely upon you, as upon Our own hands, and We desire you to look upon Us as your Head, so that the relation between Us may be one of absolute and sincere confidence and trust. Whether We perform Our duty or not, depends entirely on the manner in which you perform yours. If Our country fails to stand high in the opinion of other nations, We desire you to share in Our sorrow. If it rises with honor, We will enjoy the fruits of it with you. Stand firm in your duty: assist Us in protecting the country; and the result must be the prosperity of the nation, and the enhancement of Our country's reputation.

This is not all We wish to say to you. We have more advice for you, as follows: —

1. The principal duty of soldiers is loyalty to Sovereign and Country. It is not probable that any one born in this country will be wanting in patriotism; but for soldiers this virtue is so essential that unless a man be strong in patriotism he will be unfitted for this service. Disloyal men are like dolls, however expert and skillful they may be in their military art and science; and a troop which is well trained and led, but lacks patriotism, is like a band without a chief. The protection of the country and the maintenance of its prestige must rest upon Our military and naval forces: their efficiency or deterioration must affect, for good or for ill, the fate of Our nation; and it is therefore your duty not to entangle yourselves with social matters or political questions, but strictly to confine yourselves to the observance of your principal duty, which is loyalty, remembering always that duty is heavier than a mountain (and so to be much regarded), while death is lighter than a feather (and therefore to be despised). Never spoil your good name by a violation of good faith.

2. Soldiers must be polite in their behavior and ways. In the army and navy, there are hierarchical ranks from the Marshal to the private or bluejacket which bind together the whole for purposes of command, and there are also the gradations of seniority within the same rank. The junior must obey the senior, the inferior must take orders from the superior, who transmits to them Our direct command, and inferior and junior officers and men must pay respect to their superiors and seniors, even though they be not their direct superiors and seniors. Superiors must never be haughty or proud towards those of a lower rank, and

severity of discipline must be reserved for exceptional cases. In all other cases superiors must treat those beneath them with kindness and especial clemency, so that all men may unite as one man in the service of the country. If you do not observe courtesy of behavior, if inferiors treat their superiors with disrespect, or superiors their inferiors with harshness, if, in a word, the harmonious relations between superiors and inferiors be lost, you will be not only playing havoc with the army, but committing serious crimes against the country.

3. It is incumbent on soldiers to be brave and courageous. These two virtues have in this country been always held in very high esteem, and are indeed indispensable to Our nation: soldiers, whose profession it is to fight against the foe, should never for one instant forget that they must be brave. But there is a true bravery and a false one, which is totally different, and the rough behavior of youth cannot be called true bravery. A man of arms must always act with reason and make his plans with *sang-froid* and care. You must never despise even a small body of the enemy; on the other hand, you must never be afraid of large numbers; it is in the accomplishment of duty that true bravery lies. Those who thus appreciate true bravery will always behave with moderation towards others and will earn the respect of all men. If you act with violence you are not truly brave, and will be hated by others like a tiger or a wolf.

4. Soldiers are required to be faithful and righteous. Faithfulness and righteousness are among the ordinary duties of men: the man of arms can scarcely exist in the army without them. By the former is meant

the keeping of one's word, by the latter, the accomplishment of duty. Hence, if you wish to be faithful and righteous, you must first consider whether a thing may be done or not. If you promise to do something the nature of which is uncertain, and so entangle yourself with others, you will be in an embarrassing situation which may drive you to become unfaithful or unrighteous; and in such a case you will have no remedy, but only vain regrets.

Before embarking on any action, you must first consider whether it is right or wrong to do such a thing, and then take a firm stand upon reason. If you have reason to think that you cannot keep your word, or that the duty is too heavy, it will be wise if you refrain from action. The history of all ages gives us examples of the truth of this: many great men and heroes have perished or dishonored themselves by trying to be faithful and righteous in small things and mistaking fundamental reason, or by observing individual faithfulness at the expense of justice. You must take heed not to fall in this way.

5. It is incumbent upon soldiers to be simple and frugal. If you do not observe simplicity and frugality, you will become weak and false-hearted, and accustom yourself to luxurious habits which lead to cupidity. In that case your mind will become ignoble, and neither your loyalty nor your bravery will avail to save you from the contempt and hatred of your fellow men. This is one of the greatest sources of human misery, and if this evil be once allowed to seize hold of the army and navy, it will promptly spread like an epidemic, and all *esprit de corps* and discipline will be broken through.

We have been very much concerned about this, and have issued disciplinary regulations designed for the prevention of luxury; and now Our constant concern leads Us to tender you this advice which We desire you to keep in mind.

The above Five Articles must never for a moment be neglected by you, and you will require a true heart to put them into practice. The Five Articles are the spirit of the man of arms, and the true heart is the spirit of the Five Articles. If the heart be not true, good words and good conduct are nothing but useless external ornaments. If the heart be true, you can accomplish everything.

The Five Articles form indeed the ordinary path of human society, and there is nothing in them that cannot be easily practiced and observed.

If you serve Our country in accordance with this Our Advice you will give satisfaction not only to the Nation but to Ourselves.

APPENDIX C

IMPERIAL PROCLAMATION OF WAR

WE, by the Grace of Heaven, Emperor of Japan, seated on the Throne occupied by the same Dynasty from time immemorial, do hereby make proclamation to all Our loyal and brave subjects as follows: —

We hereby declare war against Russia and We command our army and navy to carry on hostilities against that Empire with all their strength, and We also command all Our competent authorities to make every effort in pursuance of their duties, and in accordance with their powers, to attain the national aim with all the means within the limits of the law of nations.

We have always deemed it essential to international relations and made it our constant aim to promote the pacific progress of Our Empire in civilization, to strengthen Our friendly ties with other states, and to establish a state of things which would maintain enduring peace in the Extreme East and assure the future security of Our Dominion without injury to the rights and interests of other Powers. Our competent authorities have also performed their duties in obedience to Our will, so that our relations with the Powers have been steadily growing in cordiality. It was thus entirely against Our expectation that we have unhappily come to open hostilities against Russia.

The integrity of Korea is a matter of constant concern to this Empire, not only because of Our traditional relations with that country, but because the separate existence of Korea is essential to the safety of Our Realm. Nevertheless, Russia, in disregard of her solemn treaty pledges to China, her repeated assurances to other Powers, is still in occupation of Manchuria and has consolidated and strengthened her hold upon three provinces, and is bent upon their final annexation. And since the absorption of Manchuria by Russia would render it impossible to maintain the integrity of Korea and would in addition compel the abandonment of all hope for peace in the Extreme East, We determined in those circumstances to settle the question by negotiation, and to secure thereby permanent peace. With that object in view, Our competent authorities, by Our order, made proposals to Russia, and frequent conferences were held during the course of six months. Russia, however, never met such proposals in a spirit of conciliation, but by her wanton delays put off the settlement of the question and by ostensibly advocating peace on the one hand while she was on the other extending her naval and military preparations, sought to accomplish her own selfish designs.

We cannot in the least admit that Russia had from the first any serious or genuine desire for peace. She has rejected the proposals of Our Government; the safety of Korea is in danger, the vital interests of Our Empire are menaced. The guarantees for the future which We have failed to secure by peaceful negotiations We can only now seek by an appeal to arms.

It is Our earnest wish that by the loyalty and valor of Our faithful subjects, peace may soon be permanently restored and the glory of Our Empire preserved.

[Imperial Sign Manual.]

[Privy Seal.]

February 10, 1904.

[Signed by the Minister of State.]